God's
Vitamin "C"

for the *Hurting* *Spirit*™

Compiled by
Kathy Collard Miller
and D. Larry Miller
Best-selling Authors of *God's Vitamin "C" for the Spirit*

STARBURST PUBLISHERS

P. O. Box 4123, Lancaster, Pennsylvania 17604

Kathy Collard Miller and **D. Larry Miller** speak nationally and internationally, both as individuals and together, at couple's retreats and other events. Also, Larry speaks at men's events and Kathy at women's. Larry has been involved in law enforcement for over 25 years and currently works for an Orange County, California, law enforcement agency.

Kathy is the author of 29 books, including *Healing the Angry Heart*, *Help for Hurting Moms*, *Your View of God . . . God's View of You*, *Sure Footing in a Shaky World*, and the *Daughters of the King* Bible study series. She has written over 100 published articles for *Decision*, *L.A. Times*, *Christian Parenting Today*, *Today's Christian Woman*, *Virtue*, and many other magazines. She is a contributing editor for *The Christian Communicator* and teaches at writers' seminars. As a part of the teaching staff of Christian Leaders, Authors, Speakers Seminar (CLASS), Kathy offers techniques and skills for effective communication on the platform.

Kathy and Larry have told their exciting and dynamic story of a healed marriage on numerous radio and TV programs. In addition, Kathy has shared on the 700 Club and many other radio and TV programs about being delivered from being an abusive mother.

They can be reached for scheduling speaking engagements at P.O. Box 1058, Placentia, California 92670 (714) 993-2654.

To schedule Author appearances write:
Author Appearances, Starburst Promotions, P.O. Box 4123
Lancaster, Pennsylvania 17604 or call (717) 293-0939

Credits:
Cover by David Marty Design
Unless otherwise noted, or paraphrased by the author, all Scripture quotations are from the *New International Version* of The Holy Bible.

GOD'S VITAMIN "C" FOR THE HURTING SPIRIT

First Printing, November 1997

ISBN: 0-914984-69-1
Library of Congress Catalog Number 97-068724
Printed in the United States of America

Table Of Contents

God's Vitamin "C" for the Hurting Spirit is the latest in the best-selling *God's Vitamin "C" for the Spirit* series. This collection of real-life stories expresses the breadth and depth of God's love for us in our times of need. It includes rejuvenating and inspiring thoughts from some of the most-loved Christian writers such as, Max Lucado, Cynthia Heald, Charles Swindoll and Barbara Johnson. Topics include: Death, Divorce/Separation, Financial Loss and Physical Illness.

The best-selling **God's Vitamin "C" for the Spirit**™ series also includes:

God's Vitamin "C" for the Spirit
God's Chewable Vitamin "C" for the Spirit
God's Vitamin "C" for the Spirit of MEN
God's Chewable Vitamin "C" for the Spirit of DADs
God's Vitamin "C" for the Spirit of Women
God's Chewable Vitamin "C" for the Spirit of MOMs
God's Vitamin "C" for the Christmas Spirit

See pages 269-272 for more information

1

Disability

That is why, for Christ's sake, I delight in weaknesses, in insults, in hardships, in persecutions, in difficulties. For when I am weak, then I am strong.

II Corinthians 12:10

Kinder Than Kind

When the Francis Schaeffer film and book *How Shall We Then Live?* hit Chicago in the 1970's, I joined the more than 4,000 others who were at the Aerie Crown Theater at McCormick Place to see the film.

Dr. Schaeffer was also there in person, and at end of the film, the great Christian philosopher and thinker took questions from the audience.

At one point a young man in the balcony began a question in a halting, nearly incoherent growl. Clearly, he suffered from cerebral palsy. Dr. Schaeffer closed his eyes in concentration as the question went on and on. I understood maybe one-fourth of the words.

When the man finished, Dr. Schaeffer said, "I'm sorry. I didn't understand the last three words."

The young man repeated them. "Forgive me," Dr. Schaeffer said, "The last word again, please."

After the young man repeated it, Dr. Schaeffer restated his question and answered it with the time and dignity he had accorded all the other questions. When the young man asked yet another lengthy question, some in the audience shook their heads, as if irritated that he should take so much time.

But Dr. Schaeffer repeated the process, being sure he understood every word and answered the question to completion. It struck me that he had been kinder than the occasion called for. He could have asked someone else to interpret for him. He could have asked to speak to the young man later. But everything he had expounded in his book and film was tested by this seemingly insignificant incident.

He had been kinder than kind.

A few years ago, my wife and I attended a writers conference. We were in the cafeteria, conversing with a local pastor and his wife, when a lady with cerebral palsy was wheeled to the table and her tray of food set before her.

The pastor greeted her as if her joining us was a highlight of his day. He introduced her all around and joked with her. Somehow it came out that they had met just two days before.

The rest of us sat there trying to avoid embarrassing her, not looking as she awkwardly pushed the food around on her plate, spilled most of it on its way to her mouth, and left most of that on her face. Her new friend, the pastor, took it in stride.

He didn't look away. Without fanfare he casually put his own spoon at the edge of her plate so she could scoop her mashed potatoes without losing them. He looked at her when he talked to her, and when too much food accumulated on her face, he casually wiped it away with his own napkin.

He would have been kind to have simply included her, talked to her, and treated her as a peer. But he had nurtured her, protected her, helped her without making a show of it. He had been kinder than kind.

—Jerry Jenkins

The Incredible Risk

Marrying Ray Franz was a dream come true. Tears of gratitude spilled over my lower eyelids on July 3, 1987 as we stood in a circle with his two young daughters. I hadn't dared hope I would have a husband, let alone a family.

I'd been married before for eight years—when I was diagnosed with Multiple Sclerosis. I thought our love would carry us through anything. But several years later, within a few month's time my husband left the pastorate, Ph.D. seminary studies, and me. He was having an affair with a girlfriend of mine. His betrayal tore at the very core of my being. I felt like a grain of sand under a heavy shoe, and I nearly took my life during the months of rejection. I clung to God by my fingernails, as if hanging from a cliff over the Grand Canyon.

After fifteen years of marriage my husband filed for a divorce I didn't want. A friend asked how I could trust God after what my husband had done. I told her, "Just as all of us have free choice to accept or reject Jesus, we have free choice daily whether to follow his leading or go our own way. God hasn't let me down. A human has." A year later my husband apologized for nearly destroying me as a person, as well as destroying our marriage, but he didn't seek to renew our relationship.

Piece-by-piece, the Lord put me back together again, as if with super glue. I began telling of God's trustworthiness through a speaking and singing ministry. But whenever someone asked if there was a new man in my life—I replied, "I need time." What I really needed was to believe there could be a trustworthy man.

Several years after the divorce, as a friend and I ambled from the parking lot into a single's breakfast, a tall, good-looking stranger joined us. We chatted for a few minutes. The next Sunday, he made a point of conversing with me at the break.

The following evening, as I played my newly-composed songs for my friend, Anne, the phone's trill interrupted us. "Hi, I'm

Ray Franz from the single's breakfast. We talked yesterday, remember? I wonder if you'd like to see a movie with me." I kindly asked to return his call and made my way back to the piano bench.

"Anne, I don't even know this guy!"

"Jo, it's not as if you can interview him first!"

But I did. Ray and I interviewed each other for forty-five minutes, discovering we both enjoyed biking, "I ride a tandem with a friend in the front." We both enjoyed hiking, "I used to backpack. Though I now need to rest frequently, I hike every chance I get." And we both enjoyed skiing. "Have you ever seen someone use outriggers—the skis attached to crutches? I use them, but God has blessed me with the ability to ski well." I could tell Ray wasn't getting something. "You do know I have MS, don't you?"

When Ray asked, "No, what's that?" my countenance fell. After explaining the disease, I offered Ray a way out of the date, but he wanted to go ahead. I was especially intrigued to hear Ray was a single parent, having raised his daughters for six years.

During the next week, Ray lunched with a business associate whose wife had MS. "Ray, I don't really know how strong you are emotionally. My wife is the joy of my life, but I won't kid you, the MS has made life incredibly difficult at times. I'd advise you, in your situation, don't date this woman."

We talked non-stop for six hours on our first date. Within days, we had dinner with his girls. Melissa, then seven, looked up into my eyes, beseeching, "Will you be my new Mommy?" Ray's ruddy complexion turned beet-red.

Our relationship grew quickly. The MS material I asked Ray to read was sobering, yet amazingly he said that could not be the deciding factor. "People who are healthy become ill or are injured—there are no guarantees." More significant was the fact Ray's wife had left, and I, too, had been abandoned. How does one trust another *ever* again?

Before long, we recognized solid, granite-wall commitment in one another.

One day, as Ray biked up a canyon while listening to my recording of songs called, *Victory*, he felt a peace flow over his soul like the warm breeze flowing over his body. Ray surprised me on my birthday with a proposal. God answered our individual packages of prayers with gifts of hope and promise.

Throughout these ten years, as emotional challenges threatened to tear our family apart, and physical traumas threatened to undermine our love, we've reminded each other of our commitment. Ray continues to surprise me. Recently, I found waiting at his reserved table at our favorite restaurant a bouquet of long-stemmed red roses in a vase. Each rose bud represented a year together. We're still overwhelmed with gratitude that we took the incredible risk to trust again.

—Jo Franz

Renewing Strength

Early morning on a clear July day at our farm . . . feeding our miniature horses as usual . . . almost finished . . . a sudden dizziness oozing along with a sickening weakness . . . can't hang on . . . crashing against each bar on the metal corral fence on the way to the ground . . . hitting . . . then lying still on the rock-hard ground . . . totally paralyzed as far as moving . . . the mind, eyes, ears, and voice still working . . . the yells for help failing to reach the house . . . endless minutes spent lying flat, facing the bright blue morning sky.

Thus ended my architectural career and life I had known and relished. Lying there, I prayed to my God and Savior for a full recovery. If that were not possible and I was to be a burden to those I loved, I prayed it would end right then and there. Two hawks circled and soared effortlessly overhead, perhaps as puzzled by what had happened to the man below, as was the man himself. Never before had I so wanted to take flight.

Strokes do varying degrees of damage—from no recovery to full recovery or something in between. In my case, the use of my left side came back, but my whole right side seemed doomed. I've always had faith, and so I decided to place my hope in the Lord who would renew my strength. For ten days I lived in the hospital as a broken shell with tubes attached and a regimen of shots, medications, and tests. The next thirty days were spent doing in-patient rehabilitation. With agonizing effort, my fingers and toes began twitching. Awkward and limited movement slowly returned to my arms and legs. I took my first halting steps with assistance and the use of a quad-cane. Hours of exercises built strength, coordination, and mobility.

Exhaustion set in after each therapy session, but it was apparent that my strength was coming from Him, in whom I grounded my faith.

Now, twenty months after the stroke, I can walk short distances without a cane, and have limited but improving use of my arm. I am again not only feeding the horses, but have taught my left hand to carve Native American-type drums which I sell in fine galleries. I have learned that soaring and running are very relative words. Each little step of my recovery was, to me, soaring to new heights. Each morning brought renewed strength to tackle the day's exercises. And when I was flat on my back, each halting step gained was running.

—Jerry L. Weaver

A Mother Mourns A Lost Opportunity

January 12, 1994 . . . I had so many things to do . . . grocery shopping, laundry, phone calls to return, mail to sort, unpacking. My husband and I had just returned from Germany and there was a lot of catching up needed to be done. I also had my own business and January was the last month to earn a promotional trip to Australia. A trip I was determined to earn for Gary and me. But God had other plans for my life and an important lesson for me to learn. I was exceptionally tired that day, a bad case of jet lag I thought. Tired enough that I wasn't getting my important "to-do" list accomplished. Instead, I decided to take a nap. I woke up more tired than when I went to sleep. So many things to do and so little energy . . . I dozed back to sleep.

I didn't get those things done that day nor did I get them done for the year that followed. That night I was rushed to Tri-City Hospital and spent the next four-and-a-half months there. I was diagnosed with Meningiccoccal Toxemia, a rare form of spinal meningitis that deteriorates the body's tissues and muscles.

During that time and especially in the first two months as I wavered between life and death, I had a lot of time to think about my "to-do" list. That long list of things I thought so critical. Was shopping and laundry so important? No, we had food and clean clothes in the house. How about the mail and phone calls? They would be there tomorrow. I almost died that night. How had I spent my last day?

I think I told my kids to play out back. I know I told them I was busy. When my youngest asked me to read to him, I replied "in a minute." "Can we go to the park?" asked my oldest. "Maybe tomorrow," I responded. The only problem was tomorrow almost never came. I had put on hold the really important things in life in order to accomplish the mundane and almost missed out on all that life's about.

I wished I played some ball on January 12 because for the next two months, I couldn't see my kids. I couldn't hold them close for almost a year and they couldn't sit on my lap for even longer. I'll never run with them again or play baseball or rollerblade. My legs and fingers were amputated to save my life, to stop the disease from spreading.

I'm lucky though; I got a second chance. Now when I'm asked, "Will you read to me?" I respond, "I'd love to." And when they plead "can we go to the park?" I beat them to the car—in my wheelchair.

My disability has taught me never to take anything for granted and especially not anybody. I want to grab each opportunity to make a difference in someone's life today. I've learned to spend time with the people I love. I know today is now but tomorrow may never happen. Even if it does, it may bring changes that will make a difference on what I can do. I'm not willing to take the chance. I choose to enjoy the blessings God brings my way and to make the most of each and every moment.

—Patty Kolb

Where Have All The Memories Gone?

Like a thief in the night it came creeping slowly and silently into our lives. My husband, John, who had been Master Teacher in a Southern California college, retired at the age of 78. The following summer we began to notice a change in his behavior: a missed appointment, a name or a word forgotten, a sentence left unfinished. It worsened. To the loss of memory was added confusion. It was difficult for me to believe, harder still to accept, and then to "cope."

The reality of coping came into focus at the time of the earthquake in Whittier, California. John had just put a cup of milk into the microwave to warm. As he pushed the "start" button, the earthquake hit. Walls swayed, cupboard doors flew open, dishes crashed to the floor. I ran down the hall to the kitchen. John was standing in the doorway terribly perplexed. All he could say was, "I didn't do it! I just touched the button and it exploded!" I tried to reassure him that he had done no wrong—it was an earthquake. No amount of explaining could convince him otherwise. He kept repeating, "I just touched the button."

I knew then that if I were to cope, there would need to be some changes. Our children lived on four acres near Yosemite National Park in California. I thought it might be wise to move nearer the family. My head said that was a wise decision but my heart said, "No." How could we pull up our roots at this stage in our lives and start over? Within the walls of our home I felt safe and secure.

One night I walked up and down the long hall very troubled. "I can't do it. I just can't do it! God, help me!" Calmness came. I felt wrapped in peace, like a warm blanket feels on a cold night.

I sold our home and we moved to the little guest house on our son's acreage. The little house met our every need. John was contented and so was I.

Fortunately, John did not realize that he was confused. Physically he was well. He took over the job of raking the leaves and keeping the yard neat. Thirty-nine oak trees surrounded the little house, so he never ran out of a job. However, he had to be watched carefully for often when he was tired, he would just lie down on the ground and go to sleep.

The last few years were difficult. John's memory had completely failed. He no longer knew his son, but referred to him as the "old man who lived in the big house." When his daughter came to visit and said, "Dad, do you know me?" he smiled and said, "Well, you know, I have so many students, I just can't remember all their names."

He also did not know me. One day he picked up a Bible with my name on it and said, "Now who is that?" When I told him it was I and that I was his wife, he looked perplexed and asked, "Are we legally married?" How could fifty years of marriage be so completely forgotten?

So I learned to "cope." I fixed the screen doors so he couldn't wander out at night. I hid the matches. He loved to build fires in the fireplace, but now he added too many logs.

One night he awakened and slipped out into the kitchen around 3:00 o'clock in the morning. He fixed himself breakfast. It had dry cereal, some uncooked oatmeal, peanut butter, jelly, Kitchen Bouquet, soy sauce, and chocolate powder mix. He topped it off with kernels of unpopped popcorn. I awakened in time and learned to tape the refrigerator closed and hide the popcorn.

I refused to be frustrated. I had resolved that, by God's grace, no matter what happened, I would make this my "Ha-Ha" year! Like on the day I brought the poppy-seed muffins home. I left them on the kitchen table. When I returned later I found the sink full of bits and pieces of muffins. When I questioned John, he replied, "They're all full of tiny ants." Ha! So I "coped."

One morning I awakened early. Standing on the porch I watched the sliver of a moon disappear and the sun come up. It was a beautiful spring day in May, a golden sun-shiny day. Then it happened. For a few rare moments the fog of confusion lifted from John's mind. He went out, picked five golden poppies, brought them to me and said, "You are an angel. I love you."

If you were to ask me for a definition of love, I would quickly reply, "Love is five golden poppies."

These five golden poppies were truly my legacy of love, for on May 15th, two weeks before his 93rd birthday, he awakened early and said he had a pain in his shoulder. I helped him into his robe and slippers and sat him down. He put his head against me and in a fraction of a second he was gone. He was now safely "home."

Surrounded by family and friends and busy with paper work, I did not grieve. However, grief came later when I wrote the word "widow" on a document for the first time. The finality of John's death came into focus. My hands, which had been so full of John's care, were now empty. I was determined to find a new purpose. Books had always been my friends so I decided that I, too, would write a book. I was pleasantly surprised to discover that these bits and pieces of my life were accepted and published.

True, we oldsters know that there may still be mountains to climb and a valley or two to pass through, but by God's grace we have accomplished a great feat!

Ha! Who says life is over at 83?

—Ina C. Strain

Inspired By Example

The red blossoms arching from the Christmas cactus at my kitchen window speak to me of growing old cheerfully. This is because they remind me of Martha Yake.

I first met Martha in the hospital where at age eighty-four she was recovering from a broken hip. The sparkle in her eyes and her joyful spirit grabbed my attention. *If I can be so gracious and pleasant when I am eighty-four . . .* I thought.

"What is your secret?" I asked. "How do you do it?"

Her face brightened even more as she told me, "When I entered the retirement home a few years ago I thought of my weakening physical condition and wondered what useful purpose my life could fulfill. The Lord gave me this little song, 'I'll be a Sunbeam for Jesus.' I accepted that as God's call to me and I try to live that way."

Then she pointed to a small plant in the room and asked if we would like to take it along. She didn't have a place for it back at the retirement home. We accepted it gladly as my husband and I both like plants.

My spirits soared as we left Martha's room. Usually we visit someone in the hospital to bring cheer and give gifts. But this time we received the cheer and the gift.

I cherish that kitchen window plant as it continues to remind me of Martha and her sunny disposition. Inspired by her example, I find renewed hope that I, too, can grow old cheerfully.

—Martha Denlinger Stahl

No Fear In Love

When I was a child my mother often said, "Don't stare at people, especially those who look different. You might embarrass them." I thought of that admonition one Sunday evening when my husband and I entered the foyer of the large church we attend.

There we saw a man with a normal-sized head and the body of a twelve-year-old child. Feelings of pity mingled with a hesitancy to speak to him, and, in an effort not to stare, I hurried past.

Later I noticed him sitting several rows ahead of us. As I looked at the back of his head, I recalled an incident that occurred one year when I taught second grade.

Joey, who loved to play on the swings, stopped playing there. Instead he sat at the end of our second-grade wing or followed me like a shadow during my recess duty. Finally I asked, "What's wrong, Joey? You've always liked to swing."

Drawing close to me, he whispered, "See that kid over there—the one with the hook? He wants to hurt me. He always sticks out that hook at me."

I looked toward the children from the special unit of our school. Some were in wheelchairs, some had quad canes and crutches, and others walked with difficulty. Then I saw the boy Joey meant.

"Joey, that's Danny, a new boy. He probably wants to be your friend. Why don't you stay here while I talk to him and his teacher?"

When I walked up to Danny, he extended his prosthesis and said, "Shake, Teacher!"

I shook his hook and asked him what he could do with it. Then I got his teacher's permission for Danny to come to our classroom and tell us all about it.

My second graders were wide-eyed as Danny told us he had been born with a stump of an arm and had been fitted with the prosthetic device. He wrote on the board for us, and the children giggled when he drew a funny picture of himself. Then he told us he could dress himself, could use a knife, fork, and spoon, and could even pick up jigsaw puzzle pieces. After many questions, he said, "Teacher, if your kids want to shake hands with me, I'll shake."

Joey was the first one to hold up his hand, so I let him be at the head of the line. At recess Joey ran over to Danny, shook his hook, and went on the swings with him. At the end of recess he ran up to me. "Mrs. Evans!" he exclaimed, "I'm not afraid of Danny anymore. He's my friend."

Remembering Danny, I felt remorseful for not greeting the small man and for hurrying past him. I prayed silently, "Lord, I know You love that man. In Your eyes he's no different from anyone else. Forgive me for my lack of understanding, and give me Your compassion and love for him."

At the close of the service our pastor asked all who needed prayer to raise their hands and for those nearby to pray for them. When we saw the small man's hand go up, my husband and I rushed to his side.

To several of us who gathered around him, the man introduced himself as Robert (name has been changed). He told us that he had been taking a powerful tranquilizer but felt it was wrong to become dependent on it, and so he had stopped using it. "But now I can't sleep," he said, "And I need my rest, because my schedule at the university is extremely hectic this semester."

When we prayed, compassion for the man filled my heart, and I asked the Lord to touch him and meet his deepest need.

As we continued to pray, Robert visibly relaxed and his countenance became peaceful. Then he told us he felt an overwhelming sense of God's love flooding his heart and he was at peace. "I know I'll be able to sleep well now," he concluded.

How grateful I am that the Lord enabled me to see Robert with God's eyes of love, and I pray I will never again be hesitant to reach out to people who look different.

—Marjorie K. Evans

Our Journey Into Twilight

Seventeen summers ago, Muriel and I began our journey into the twilight. It's midnight now, at least for her, and sometimes I wonder when dawn will break. Even the dread Alzheimer's disease isn't supposed to attack so early and torment so long. Yet, in her silent world, Muriel is so content, so lovable. If Jesus took her home, how I would miss her gentle, sweet presence. Yes, there are times when I get irritated, but not often. It doesn't make sense to get angry. And besides, perhaps the Lord has been answering the prayer of my youth to mellow my spirit.

Once, though, I completely lost it. In the days when Muriel could still stand and walk and we had not resorted to diapers, sometimes there were "accidents." I was on my knees beside her, trying to clean up the mess as she stood, confused, by the toilet. It would have been easier if she weren't so insistent on helping. I got more and more frustrated. Suddenly, to make her stand still, I slapped her calf—as if that would do any good. It wasn't a hard slap, but she was startled. I was, too. Never in our 44 years of marriage had I ever so much as touched her in anger or in rebuke of any kind. But now, when she needed me most . . . .

Sobbing, I pled with her to forgive me—no matter that she didn't understand words any better than she could speak them. So I turned to the Lord to tell him how sorry I was. It took me days to get over it. Maybe God bottled those tears to quench the fires that might ignite again some day.

It wasn't long before I found myself again, on the floor in the bathroom. Muriel wanted to help—hadn't cleaning up messes been her specialty? But now those busy hands didn't know exactly what to do. I mopped frantically, trying to fend off the interfering hands, and contemplated how best to get a soiled slip over a head that was totally opposed to the idea. At that moment Chuck Swindoll boomed from the radio in the kitchen, "Men! Are you at home? *Really* at home?" In the midst of my stinking immersion I smiled, "Yeah, Chuck, I really am." Do I ever wish I weren't?

What some people find so hard to understand is that loving Muriel isn't hard. They wonder about my former loves—like my work. A college freshman heard that I had resigned as president of Columbia International University to care for my wife. "Do you miss being president?" Scott asked as we sat in our little garden. I told him I'd never thought about it, but, on reflection, no. As exhilarating as my work had been, I enjoyed learning to cook and keep house. No, I'd never looked back.

But that night I did reflect on his question and turned to the Lord. "Father, I like this assignment, and I have no regrets. But if a coach puts a man on the bench, he must not want him in the game. You needn't tell me, of course, but I'd like to know—why didn't you need me in the game?"

I didn't sleep well that night and awoke contemplating the puzzle. Muriel was still mobile at that time, so we set out on our morning walk around the block. She wasn't too sure on her feet, so we went slowly and held hands as we always do. This day I heard footsteps behind us and looked back to see the familiar form of a local derelict. He staggered past us, then turned and looked us up and down. "Tha's good. I likes 'at," he said. "Tha's real good. I likes it."

He turned and headed back down the street, mumbling to himself over and over, "Tha's good. I likes it."

When Muriel and I reached our garden and sat down, his words came back to me. Then the realization hit me; the Lord had spoken through an inebriated old derelict. "It is you who are whispering to my spirit, 'I likes it, tha's good,'" I said aloud. "I may be on the bench, but if you like it and say it's good, that's all that counts."

Then came February 14, 1995.

Valentine's Day was always special at our house because that was the day in 1948 when Muriel accepted my marriage proposal. On the eve of Valentine's Day in 1995, I read a statement by some specialist that Alzheimer's is the most cruel disease of all, but that the victim is actually the caregiver. I wondered why I never felt like a victim. That night I entered in my journal: "The reason I don't feel like a victim is—I'm not!" When others urged me to call it quits, I responded, "Do you realize how lonely I would be without her?"

After I bathed Muriel on her bed that Valentine's eve and kissed her good night (she still enjoys two things: good food and kissing!), I whispered a prayer over her: "Dear Jesus, you love sweet Muriel more than I, so please keep my beloved through the night; may she hear the angel choirs."

The next morning I was peddling on my Exercycle at the foot of her bed and reminiscing about some of our happy lovers' days long gone while Muriel slowly emerged from sleep. Finally, she popped awake and, as she often does, smiled at me. Then, for the first time in months she spoke, calling out to me in a voice clear as a crystal chime, "Love . . . love . . . love." I jumped from my cycle and ran to embrace her. "Honey, you really do love me, don't you?" Holding me with her eyes and patting my back, she responded with the only words she could find to say : "I'm nice;" she said.

Those may prove to be the last words my wife will ever speak.

—Robertson McQuilkin

Born Different

When Shirleyan Johnson stands in front of an audience to speak or sing, it doesn't take long for people to discover that she is different. If she holds a microphone, they see only one little finger curled around it—or two, if she uses both hands. If they are sharp eyed, they notice her shoes are not the latest style. Pointed to accommodate one toe on each foot, they resemble Grandma's sturdy footwear.

Shirleyan never says in public, "I'm handicapped." Though she publicly admits she is different, she never had to re-learn to do things. Her way is normal, for her. But this hasn't always been her attitude.

For years she struggled, pretending that being born with only one digit on each hand and foot didn't exist, or that it was only temporary. As a child, she thought that God had mislaid some parts and would some day take care of the problem. She wouldn't accept her mother's statement, "This is God's plan. Some day it will be a blessing."

When Shirleyan invited Jesus Christ into her life at an early age, she expected to become happy and whole overnight. It didn't happen, and she refused to accept that it was God's will to make her different. She questioned, *Why God? Why me? If my defects are a blessing, why not my older sister? After all she is the firstborn.* But she received no answer, and she determined to face a hostile world with all the might she could muster.

With prosthetic aids in her shoes, Shirleyan learned to walk—contrary to her doctor's predictions. Yet she envied her sisters their open-toed sandals and their ability to run barefoot.

Shirleyan grew up fighting to prove that she could do all the things everyone else could. She played the piano, sang in the church choir, and played trombone in the marching band at school.

However, though the Lord gave her a talent for singing,

Shirleyan refused invitations to sing in churches other than her own because she couldn't face public curiosity. ✗✗

Then one day her pastor called her into his study. Kind, but frank, he said, "Shirleyan, you'll never be happy until you accept and adjust to your condition."

Shirleyan rushed home, expecting sympathy from her parents, but they agreed with the pastor. This increased Shirleyan's determination to become independent.

She went to college, intending to major in education. There she met Gary Johnson. When Gary first asked Shirleyan for a date, she didn't know what to say. She hid her hands behind her back, convinced Gary would change his mind when he saw them. But Gary persisted and they began dating. However, Shirleyan was still skeptical. She thought, *Naturally, his interest is purely scientific because he's a biology major.*

Then one day, Gary asked her to meet him in the college chapel. She thought, *Here it comes, the friendly brush-off.* Instead, he asked her to marry him. Although Shirleyan loved him and wanted to accept, she hesitated until Gary stated, "God has chosen you for me."

Shirleyan wished she could say "we lived happily ever after" but God still had to teach her to accept His will in making her different. The initial test came when Scott, her first son, was born—with the same physical defect as his mother's.

In bitterness, Shirleyan reproached God, *Wasn't it enough to make me the way I am? Why my child, too?* She had thought God would prove His love for her by giving her a perfect baby. ✗✗

The Johnsons attended Gary's home church in Phoenix at the time. When the pastor called Shirleyan into his office to talk, she thought, *Here we go again.* She was right. The pastor gave her an attitude check, then prescribed I Thessalonians 5:16-18. At home, Shirleyan concentrated on verse 18: *This is the will of God in Christ Jesus concerning you.* She fell on her knees and at last accepted God's plan for her life. "All right, God," she prayed, "If you're really there, and you can use my life, I'm yours."

Then the Johnsons' second son, Eric, was born—with Shirleyan's same physical defect. Although disappointed, she accepted it. And God's pure peace filled her beyond understanding.

She received invitations to speak and sing, and once again her stubborn will battled against God's leading. But as she saw the Lord glorified, her self-consciousness decreased. By word of mouth only, Shirleyan soon received invitations for an average of four engagements a week, visiting churches, schools and camps. Since she worked five days a week, she had to rely solely on God's strength, and He proved faithful every time.

Shirleyan tried to protect her sons, and kept them from public view as much as possible. But, like the Baby Moses, they could only be hidden for a while. She learned that you can't tuck a teenage boy under a baby blanket!

Under Gary's patient coaching, the boys learned to play soccer. Each of them learned to play the trombone. Sharing their mother's love of singing, they joined her in some of her concerts.

God continues to work on Shirleyan's stubborn streak and strong will. When she travels, someone frequently offers to help with her luggage. She would rather handle it herself, but God reminds her to accept the help, even if it is offered in pity.

At some point in her program, she accompanies herself on the piano, not to show off her ability to play, but to emphasize what God can do with an imperfect vessel. Using small nubs that resemble knuckles on each hand, she is able to play so that only those with trained ears detect omitted notes.

Time and again Shirleyan has seen God bless others as she shares what He has done in her life. Day by day, she is discovering why she was born different.

—Mildred Barger

Resisting Temptation

I'll never forget the first day of my marriage to Ken. What a carefree, delightful morning!

As our jet lifted off from Los Angeles to fly us to our honeymoon in Hawaii, we cuddled and kissed. The flight attendants giggled and presented us with a cake and a couple of leis. After they served refreshments, we settled back and put on the earphones to watch the in-flight movie. To my surprise it was *Whose Life Is It Anyway?*, the film about a quadriplegic who tried to get everyone from his friends to his doctor to his lawyer to permit him the right to die.

Ken and I pulled off our earphones. This was not the time to think about the depression of quadriplegia or the desire it often brings to cut one's life short.

As the opening credits appeared on the screen, the flight attendant knelt by my seat and whispered, "Oh, Mrs. Tada, I'm very sorry about the movie selection today. Shall we change your seat?"

I smiled and shook my head no. I knew I had hope and a future, although I had a difficult time the rest of the flight convincing the attendants that I was not bothered by the visual images on the screen. Yet, even as Ken and I snuggled and talked of our future, I kept sneaking peeks at the film.

Without the soundtrack, strange and twisted thoughts began to whisper and wheedle into my brain. *Does Ken really know what he's gotten himself into? What if we can't handle it? Divorce and suicide happen to couples like us all the time. What if . . . .*

Hold it! This was the happiest day of my life, and I refused to entertain such deplorable thoughts! I shook my head, jerked my attention away from the movie, and riveted it totally on Ken. I wasn't about to allow subtle ideas, like flying birds, to build a nest in my head.

It's called resisting temptation.

—Joni Eareckson Tada

Just Because I Love You

Autumn lay like a copper blanket at my doorstep and old wood smoke and memories filled the air. A reminder that all things come to an end. The little girl in me shuffled through golden coins of birch leaves lying in the driveway as I picked fiery maples for the table.

But I wasn't a little girl anymore. Mother was the little girl now. Decisions, questions, packing, filled my days.

I took a deep breath and ran into the house. I lay the leaves on the table beside bronze candles remembering how Mom always admired and displayed the many bouquets and branches I brought to her through all those growing up years.

I needed her this morning and gathered her music box into my arms and felt the comfort of the words, "Oh, what a beautiful morning." Momma bunny in her flowered straw hat and apron, her tail tied with pink ribbons, sprinkling glazed ceramic petunias with her watering can. Around and around she went, the music filling the room and me. A gift from my daughter to Mother. "For no reason, Grandma. Just because I love you," she had said.

When Mom was unable to keep her large home anymore, we moved her to an apartment. Mrs. Rabbit and the music went with her. And when her mind began to slip away, we stopped daily, taking meals and chatting, hoping to keep her alert and functioning. Sun spots danced across the table top as I fixed Mom's tray and added a fresh bouquet of cosmos and daisies. At breakfast, I wound the music spring and before I left Mom always wound it for me. When I took dinner in, I smiled and set the music box beside her tray thinking, yes, what a beautiful day. Then I turned on Lawrence Welk and the champagne bubbles which always brought light to her eyes, and she talked about the old songs, how Dad, gone 25 years now, sang them to her over and over.

Then things began to change again and the days filled with

the flat colors of grief as we moved Mother to assisted living because of medical needs and her mind slipping further away. Still I played the music box for her when I visited. But she stopped playing it for me, blamed my brother and me for her situation, unable to understand her need for care and safety.

She no longer smiled in recognition when I wound the music box. "Take it away," she said. "And don't smile at me, you're two faced."

Some days were good, some very bad. I continued to go but took the music box home and retired it to a shelf, gathering dust like Mother's mind.

October again, and the changing of seasons and our lives: I asked Mom if she would like to go for a ride through the leaves. "No," she said blankly. So the next day I brought her a bright crimson and yellow branch of maple leaves with the last of my roses. For a dozen years I had sent her leaves in the mail each autumn and she displayed them in saran wrap on the side of her refrigerator in the old house with the date each year and a sign. "Leaves from Doris."

Today there was a spark of recognition as I put the bouquet on her dresser. "I wonder if you know how much you're missed," she said. "I smiled and buttoned her coat and tied her shoes. Her sad eyes met mine. "You shouldn't have to do that." I patted her leg, "I want to, and you certainly tied shoes a long time for me."

We drove down to a family gathering and she enjoyed the scenery but the noise of the world unnerved her. I turned up the radio to drown out the traffic and sang along. "God made the ivy to twine, God made the sun and stars to shine, God made you mine, that's why I love you." I reached over and squeezed her hand and saw silent tears sliding down her cheeks. "It's so much fun to have you with me, Mom. Remember when I was learning to drive and you let me take you everywhere? After eggs and milk? And picking up sewing for you? How did you ever have time to make so many pretty things for all of us kids too?"

She smiled as I continued. "I remember especially my yellow pinafore at Easter, and you found enough money for me to go to the church breakfast too. And the shoes, white with straps. I lay them on my pillow so I could smell the new leather beside me all night. But I knew that you needed shoes much more than me."

I saw a glint of remembering in her eyes and I sang the song I always sang to her through the years. "Everywhere you go, sunshine always follows you." She reached over and patted my arm.

She pointed out the window. "The leaves are pretty."

"Yes," I answered, "I love autumn and the crops. You always said not to shake the apples on the tree but to wait for one to fall. We used to swing on the bars and pump high in the old rope swing, with one ear listening for the sound of a ripe, sweet apple about to hit the ground."

Everyone came out to greet us at the dinner. Mom was too nervous to stay long, but had a chance to see her great grand-children.

I never knew the response each time I pushed open the double doors to the Alzheimer's section of the nursing home we finally had to move her to. I wanted more for my mother in her last days. I also had wanted more from her as I was growing up. But she gave all she knew how to give. And there are things we cannot change.

I had long forgotten about the music box, but dusting it one day, I decided to take it on my next visit. She was asleep when I arrived and patted her shoulder. "Hi Mom, I brought you a gingerbread cookie."

She sat up slowly and smiled. I briefed her on all the family and she remembered some of them.

I took a deep breath, wound the music box and set it on her dresser. Her eyes, clouded with tears, and she began to sing. "Oh, what a beautiful morning."

I wound it again and brought it closer to her. "Would you like me to bring it next to the bed?"

She nodded and pulled me close as we sat on the bed together.

We chatted enjoying the fresh autumn breeze from her window, then I tucked her in for a nap before dinner. She fell asleep quickly on her side, her fleshy face folding in against her nose, and I smoothed the curls of her new perm into a pixie look around her ear. As I turned to go back out into the world, shadows danced across the bulletin board filled with the faces of my brothers and sisters and our families. Her breath rose and fell in rhythm as I backed the rest of the way out of the room, the music box under my arm. I blew her a silent kiss, felt a low hum inside me, and saw that the shape of a leaf lay on her cheek—and didn't go away.

—Doris Hays Toppen

2

Memories

For everything that was written in the past was written to teach us, so that through endurance and the encouragement of the Scriptures we might have hope.

Romans 15:4

Dachau Chaplain

At the Protestant Chapel on the grounds of the Dachau concentration camp near Munich, I met with an amazing man who survived the Holocaust and now has taken on a life mission of announcing to the world that God's love is deeper than the sloughs of human depravity. He helped me understand how Corrie's (Corrie Ten Boom) view of life is possible during such a time.

The man, Christian Reger, spent four years as a prisoner in Dachau. His crime? He had belonged to the Confessing Church, the branch of the German state church which opposed Hitler (two of its leaders were Martin Niernoeller and Dietrich Bonhoeffer). Reger was turned over to authorities by his church organist and shipped hundreds of miles away to Dachau.

I met Reger on the grounds of the Dachau camp. The International Dachau Committee, of which Reger is a leader, has worked to restore the camp as a monument so the world cannot forget. "Never Again" is their slogan.

I found Reger in the Protestant Chapel which stands near a Catholic convent and a Jewish memorial. He wanders the grounds, searching out tourists, conversing with them in German, English, and French, answering questions, reminiscing about his inmate days. He tells of the final winter, when coal supplies were low and the ovens were finally shut off. Prisoners no longer had the constant stench of burning comrades hanging over the camp. Then, dead bodies were stacked naked in the snow like cordwood, a number stenciled on each with a blue marker.

Christian Reger will tell the horror stories if you ask. But he will never stop there. He goes on to share his faith—how at Dachau he was visited by a God who loves.

"Nietzsche said a man can undergo torture if he knows the why of his life," Reger told me. "But I, here at Dachau, learned something far greater. I learned to know the Who of my life. He was enough to sustain me then, and is enough to sustain me still."

It was not always so. After his first month in Dachau, Reger had, like Elie Wiesel, abandoned all hope in a loving God. The odds against His existence, from the perspective of a Nazi prisoner, were just too great. Then, in July, 1941, something happened to challenge his doubt. Prisoners were allowed only one letter a month, and exactly one month from the date of his incarceration, Christian Reger received the first news from his wife. The letter, carefully clipped in pieces by censors, chatted about the family and her love for him. At the bottom, was printed a reference to Bible verses: Acts 4:26-29. Reger looked up the verses, part of a speech by Peter and John after being released from prison.

The kings of the earth take their stand, and the rulers gather together against the Lord and against his Anointed One. Indeed Herod and Pontius Pilate met together with the Gentiles and the people of Israel in this city to conspire against your holy servant Jesus, whom you anointed. They did what your power and will had decided beforehand should happen. Now, Lord, consider their threats and enable your servants to speak your word with great boldness.

That afternoon Reger was to face interrogators, the most frightening experience in the camp. He would be called on to name fellow Christians, and if he gave in to pressures, those Christians would be captured and possibly killed. There was a good chance he would be beaten with clubs or tortured with electricity if he refused to cooperate with the interrogation. The verses meant little to him. What possible help could God be at a time like this?

Reger moved to the waiting area outside the interrogation room. He was trembling. The door opened, and a fellow minister whom Reger had never met came out. Without looking at Reger or changing the expression on his face, he walked to him, slipped something into Reger's coat pocket, and walked away. Seconds later SS guards appeared and ushered Reger inside the room. The interrogations went well; they were surprisingly easy and involved no violence.

When Reger arrived back at the barracks, he was sweating

from tension. He breathed deeply for several moments, trying to calm himself, then crawled into his bunk, covered with straw. Suddenly he remembered the strange incident with the other minister. He reached in his pocket and pulled out a matchbox. *Oh*, he thought, *what a kind gesture. Matches are a priceless commodity in the barracks.* Inside, however, there were no matches, just a folded slip of paper. Reger unfolded the paper, and his heart pounded hard against his chest. Neatly printed on the paper was this reference: Acts 4:26-29.

It was a miracle, a message from God. There was no way that minister could have seen his letter from his wife—he did not even know the minister. God had arranged the event as a demonstration that He was still alive, still able to strengthen, still worthy of trust.

Christian Reger was transformed from that moment. It was a small miracle, as miracles go, but it was enough to found his faith in bedrock that could not be jarred by the atrocities, murders, and human injustice he would see the next four years in Dachau.

"God did not rescue me and make my suffering easier. He simply proved to me that He was still alive, and He still knew I was here. We Christians drew together. We formed a church here, among other convicted pastors and priests—a forced ecumenical movement, we called it. We found our identity as one flesh, as part of Christ's body."

"I can only speak for myself. Others turned from God because of Dachau. Who am I to judge them? I simply know that God met me. For me, He was enough, even at Dachau."

As long as he has health, Christian Reger will stiffly pace the grounds of Dachau, speaking to tourists in his warm, accented voice. He will tell them what it was like and where God was during the long night at Dachau.

—Philip Yancey

The Last Walk

The call came unexpectedly late one evening. As I listened to the voice on the other end, tears began to pool in my eyes and a wave of guilt washed over me. "Okay, Dad, I understand. I'll be there as soon as I can," was the only reply I could squeak out. A few more details and the conversation ended. I hung up the phone. No longer needing to restrain myself, I began to weep. Softly at first and then harder as I felt my husband's arms slip around me.

"Laura, what's wrong?"

I managed to explain between sobs, "My dad says my grandma is in the hospital with pneumonia and the doctors don't think she's going to make it."

"You need to get on a plane and go see her right away," he instructed.

"I know," I responded, panic now rising in my voice, "But what do you say to someone you haven't seen in fifteen years?"

I had let so much time pass since seeing my grandparents. I searched my memory for remnants from my last visit with them—the summer I was sixteen-years-old. But nothing came to me. The thousands of miles that separated us no longer seemed like justification for not visiting, or the fact that college had kept me "too busy," then marriage, children and life in general. I felt ashamed. How could I face her now? Maybe I shouldn't go. She probably thinks I don't even care about her. A restlessness inside told me I was wrong. This time nothing else seemed as important as seeing Grandma again.

On the airplane I closed my eyes and tried to remember the little whitewashed house with the brick steps where my grandparents still lived. I could picture the lush green yard where my brothers and I used to run and play during summer vacations. I saw the pink blossoms on the cherry trees that dotted their property and thought I could even smell Grandma's mouth-watering cherry pies baking in the oven. There was something else I loved about going to Grandma's—what was it? It was something we did together, but I couldn't remember . . . .

The pilot's voice on the intercom announcing our descent into Des Moines shattered my thoughts and the hope of any more recollection was lost in the drone of the engines. I sighed wearily and began to collect my things.

My legs felt like lead as I stepped from the car and entered the front doors of the hospital. The faint smell of death curled at my nose and I shook my head, refusing to acknowledge it. As we made the trek down the long corridors to Grandma's hospital room, I began to pray, "Lord, I need you to help me. I don't know what to say to Grandma. Somehow Lord, I need to let her know that I love her. That I have always loved her even in my absence. Please give me the words."

As I finished my prayer, I found myself standing outside the door to Grandma's room. I stood there for a few moments, watching the steady rise and fall of her chest. She was so thin I could see her heart beating through her hospital gown. As I lingered in the doorway I heard a whisper. Though faint, the words were very real. "You don't need to say anything. Your being here is enough. She has been waiting for you."

That assurance stirred my courage and I took a few steps into the room. Grandma's head turned toward the doorway and a faint smile appeared on her lips. "There you are," she said extending a hand. "I've been waiting for you."

Smiling back, I took her hand and sat on the edge of her bed, gazing into her soft hazel eyes. She was just as I had remembered, only more frail, and tired. As I bent to hug her, I began to cry softly. But the tears were no longer those of fear or guilt, but of joy, the kind you cry when you see an old friend after a very long time, and she was sharing them with me.

After awhile we dried our eyes and began to talk. She seemed to be filled with a new energy as she spoke of years past and my childhood visits. There was a softness in her words, a sweetness in her eyes, and I realized that she harbored no ill feelings toward my absence.

We spent the next few days that way. Although I felt at peace being there with her, there was still something troubling me. It was a memory, lingering behind a closed door that I couldn't get open.

On the last day of my visit she patted my hand and looking out the window said, "remember our walks?" Our walks! The words sprung at me and something inside my head clicked as a door from the past flew open.

"Oh, yes," I began excitedly as the memory became clearer, "We used to go for walks every night after supper!"

Her eyes seemed to sparkle as she recalled, "I loved those walks with you. We'd pick wildflowers and look for squirrels and talk about anything that was on our hearts."

Yes, now I remembered. Grandma loved to walk. Down by the riverbank, through the park, along the sleepy town's streets at dusk; Grandma walked anywhere I wanted to go. Those walks were special to both of us. The look in her eyes told me she wished she could get up now and take one last walk with me—but the memories would have to do. She sighed deeply and wrapping her arms around me, then gave me another hug. Neither one of us said it, but we both knew it would be the last.

A few weeks later when I got the call that Grandma had passed away, I listened intently as my mother told me that Grandma's last words to the nurse had been that she was going for a walk with Jesus. As I hung up the phone this time I didn't cry. Instead, a smile crept over me as I thought of Grandma. She got to take that last walk after all.

—Laura Sabin Riley

My Father's Hands

My father's hands were large and rough from long hours of hard work on his farm. Here he had hammered out his philosophy of life that work is not only our lot but, also our fulfillment. As a babe in arms, he had been carried to America by Swedish emigrants. With great expectancy, they had come to this new land to build a new life.

By the time my father and mother were married, he owned twenty acres of land and had built a large two story house with his hands. My sister and I were born there and grew to maturity.

My father's lap was my place of security. Lifting me up, he drew me close to his loving heart while his hands caressed my hair and wiped my tears away. I wanted to stay there forever because I knew that I was loved, understood and accepted. Soon I must share my place with my sister or my father needed to go back to his work. My day would go on, too, but now I could cope with my problem knowing my place of comfort and security would always be there for me.

His hands that expressed love also meted out discipline. How well I remember my first spanking when I was almost four. My body was not injured but my character grew that day.

A new baby girl had been born in our family and I was sent out to play. My game of throwing rocks ended as one hit the dog's dish on the porch with a crash. Like Adam and Eve, my first thought was to hide from trouble. Quickly I crawled under the porch and lay as still as a shadow.

"Christine, where are you? Come here to me!" Father called—but I didn't move. Little girls don't disappear in thin air and soon two big hands pulled a scared and surprised little girl from her hiding place and applied the consequences of her crime.

That day I learned some of my father's values. I was sure my crime was breaking the dog's dish but he explained the spanking was for not coming when he called.

My father often took my hand and led me through the meadow to a rabbit's nest or through the woods to a neighbor's house to play. Sometimes he led me across the field to our mailbox. I was learning to walk in confidence to new places. My spirit was learning to trust a Heavenly Father who could lead me through life's pathways.

During my teen and college days, I learned to appreciate my father's hands even more. Food, clothing and school meant much hard work during the depression days of the 20's and 30's. After the farm work was done, he found time to grow flowers. His hands grew even more callused and rough as he cultivated lovely roses, lilies, dahlias and iris. His heart grew more tender and loving as he shared his flowers with family and friends.

We were so happy that we forgot to count the years. College, teaching and marriage came in sequence.

One morning, I was called to the hospital. Standing helpless by my father's bedside, I saw his body become a silent piece of clay when angel messengers carried his spirit to that home our Heavenly Father's hands have prepared for those who love Him. At seventy-eight, my earthly father lost his battle with cancer.

Standing by his casket, surrounded with the beautiful flowers that he loved so much, I saw those dear hands folded in death. Through my tears I thanked God that He had given me such a wonderful, earthly father. A father who read and believed his Bible; who had trusted the Lord Jesus as his Savior from sin; a father who loved his family, his country and his God.

Life is a scroll unfolding a day at a time. We don't see the patterns that are etched in memory until one day they are flashed back to us and we see the colors and patterns of the past. The memory of my father's hands have deepened my love for my Savior's hands that were pierced by the nails on the cross that we might see the Heavenly Father's love.

—Christine Barrett

Momma's Treasures

"This won't be easy," I said to my sister Sandra, as we drove the six blocks to Momma's house.

A lump filled my throat when we stopped in front of the small white stucco house. From my earliest childhood and even after I married and left home, the moment my foot hit the front porch, I would yell, "Momma, I'm home."

This homecoming was different. Three weeks earlier, the day before Easter, Momma lost her battle with cancer, but won the victory over death. She went home to be with the Lord.

Sandra's voice jolted me back. "We'll clean out her closets, pack her clothes, then come back later and decide what to do with the furniture and dishes."

The front door creaked when we opened it. Thick musty air hung in the room.

"Let's open some windows and sit on the porch for a while," Sandra said.

I watched her stare at Momma's rocker next to a small table which held the telephone and a worn Bible.

A heavy feeling pressed down and I gasped for air. I stumbled out the door and gulped in the freshness of the day. I sank to the cool concrete porch.

"Are you all right, Cozy?" Sandra asked. She settled beside me.

I nodded. Tears burned my eyes.

I looked at Sandra in a new light. She was the younger sister, the baby of the family, but during Momma's illness she stood firm. She took a leave from her job as a nurse and stayed with Momma. Because of Sandra, Momma never spent time in a nursing home.

I took a deep breath and savored the sweet smell of lilac mixed with honeysuckle. Red, yellow, pink, and purple flowers lined the front sidewalk and I began to laugh.

"Remember the time when you were about six and you got mad at Momma because she wouldn't let you go over to Janet's to play?"

Sandra nodded. "I stomped down the walk pulling up every one of her prized flowers. Not a one left."

"Oh, yes, there was," I interrupted. "There was a tall hollyhock and Momma pulled it and used it as a switch."

"Boy, did the stickers on that hollyhock sting."

Laughing, Sandra continued, "Remember the time she washed your mouth out with Lava soap when you used a cuss word?"

"But I didn't know it was a cuss word."

"You did after that."

A soft breeze tickled my neck. "Remember Momma's light flaky biscuits?" I asked. "And her peach cobbler?"

"Momma had a good life. Her pain and troubles are over, but her joy will last forever."

I took a deep breath and exhaled. "Look at the beauty surrounding us. Know what Momma would say right now? This is the da . . ." My voice cracked.

Sandra stood and extended her hand. "Come on, let's get in there and get busy."

Amid the tears and laughter we soon had the closets cleaned out. I sat on the edge of the bed and glanced around. A faint trace of rose talcum lingered in the room.

Sandra pulled out a drawer and brought it to the bed and dumped the contents.

"Look, Momma's purse," I said, holding up a black leather bag. I opened the latch and pulled out a holder containing pictures of my two sisters, me and all the grandkids.

Then I found a folded piece of paper with time-worn creases. Tears filled my eyes as I read the title, "My Mother." I handed it to Sandra. "I wrote this poem twenty-five years ago and sent it to Momma in a birthday card."

Before the day ended we discovered more of Momma's treasures. Beneath her bed lay a box of childish pictures colored in crayon. A shiny star graced the top of each one. Faded brittle paper revealed tiny hand prints with our names and dates. A book of poems with flowers pressed between the pages, nestled beneath our school pictures. A frayed blue ribbon bound a stack of photos—our prom pictures.

"No antique dealer is going to offer us silver and gold for Momma's treasures," I said.

Sandra opened the book with the pressed flowers. "Do you think these are the ones I pulled up?"

"Could be," I answered.

Sandra shook her head. "No antique dealer has enough money to buy momma's treasures."

I looked around Momma's small bedroom and felt the presence of the Lord. "Just think of the mansion Momma lives in now."

As we walked to the car, peace and joy filled my heart.

"Know what Momma is probably singing right now?" I asked.

Sandra smiled and we both burst out in song, "This is the day that the Lord has made . . . ."

—Helen Luecke

Respite

My father-in-law suffered a stroke one summer. Family members came from miles around to be with him. One afternoon, it was obvious he was slipping away from us. My husband's mother, Bill's eight siblings, their spouses and children gathered round Grandpa's hospital bed. The pain for those he was leaving behind was unbearable.

His heart sounds slowly faded away until there was nothing.

After an eternal silence, Mom asked us to join hands and say "The Lord's Prayer." We could hardly speak, but someone managed to begin a prayer. Without a thought, we all joined in and began to pray—Grace Before Meals.

We all stopped at once, suddenly realizing our mistake, and took a deep breath before finally submitting to a little bit of laughter. And it was good. Not only were we making a memory we'd cherish forever, but feeling his presence still, we knew Dad was delighted that he'd "left us laughing."

—**Mary Bahr Fritts**

Thanks, Mom

Silence filled the room as my mother's body lay motionless in the hospital bed. I edged closer and fluffed her beautiful silver-gray hair. *She always liked me to style her hair.*

"I'm going to make some calls in the waiting room, Sharon," my husband whispered. "Maybe you'd like some time alone with Mom."

Gently pulling the sheet down below her hands, I patted them like she had done to mine so many times. *If only her hands would reach out and hold mine once again.*

I began to talk out loud. "We're all going to miss you, Mom. When we last talked, you wanted me to be sure to tell Jennifer and Melissa how much you love them. I never dreamed those words would be the last ones you would ever speak to me."

I patted her hands again and laid my head next to her shoulder on the cool sheet. *Oh Mom, I wish we could talk together just one more time. There's so much to thank you for. Remember how your granddaughters loved your creamy oatmeal fixed "Nana's way"? I'd offer to make it but they always preferred yours. My oatmeal seemed like the "hurry-up" version with lumps! Yours was made with twenty minutes of tender loving care.*

Reminiscing came easy. "Remember last week I visited you at your home? I knocked on the door and you didn't answer. Had your aneurysm burst?"

I could visualize everything. "Mom, it's me, your baby," I had called out, standing on the steps by your back door. Saying those words was a pleasure now, especially at my age of 47! I yelled louder repeating, "It's your daughter, your baby!" Fear spread through my body. Resting my head against your locked door I heard nothing. I hoped you hadn't had another heart attack! I wasn't ready to say good-bye to my Mom! I pounded harder on your door. "Mom, it's me!" I yelled.

My mother's weak voice put my fears to rest. "I'm coming, honey."

I breathed a sigh of relief and threw my arms around her as soon as she unlocked the door.

"Come in, Sharon, I'm always glad to see you." I took her cane and held her arm close to mine as we walked to her chair next to what she called her "pill table."

"You look great, Mom."

"Oh, do I?" she replied, not quite believing me. "There's coffee in the kitchen," she added.

"No thanks, Mom. Tell me what you've been doing today."

"Not much, honey. I'm just putting all my pills in my organizer. That's such a big job for me." She started explaining what each pill was for and how many she took a day. I tried to listen attentively but thoughts of the active mother I had once known crowded my mind. Only a few years ago she had managed a successful credit union. During that time, she raised three children. I still remember the day she took my brother to a father-son football banquet when he was a high school senior. My alcoholic father missed many opportunities to share special moments with us. But Mom was always there.

I continued to watch her as she slowly placed each pill in her organizer. "If I get this job done, I'll feel I've accomplished a lot today," she said with a smile.

"Mom, you're still a sharp gal," I reassured her.

"Do you really think so?" she asked, as I placed her favorite afghan over her legs.

"Sharon, there's something I want you to know."

"You sound serious, Mom."

"I want you to know I'm at peace with God."

I smiled at her.

"I'm not afraid to die," she said. "It's just that I'm not ready to say good-bye to my children."

"I'm not ready to say good-bye to you either, Mom," I whispered as my eyes filled with tears, "But someday we'll be together forever in God's kingdom."

"Making you cry was not my intent, Sharon." She patted my hands. "I just want you to know I'm all right. I am one of His."

There was a light knock on the hospital door. I sat up reluctantly as if I had been awakened from a wonderful dream. I knew it was time to leave her.

"It's me, honey," Skip said lovingly. "Are you ready to go home?"

I smiled at Mother and patted her hands for the last time.

"Good-bye Mom—my prayer partner—my best friend. I'm going to miss you, but I know I will see you again." I kissed her cheek.

The big heavy hospital door closed quietly behind us. Skip and I put our arms around each other and walked down the hallway in silence. It was then I realized, Mom had given me the best gift I could have ever received. She shared with me the purpose of life—being "one of His." Thanks, Mom.

—**Sharon Wilkins**

3

Loss Of A Loved One

You have made known to me the path of life; you will fill me with joy in your presence, with eternal pleasures at your right hand.

Psalm 16:11

The First Day Of Summer

It was a beautiful day, this first day of Summer. The Kansas sun shone hot with the promise of the season. It was the day Mom died.

Three months previously she got the news. Cancer. Widespread throughout her body. Not treatable. I remember walking in a daze out of her house that day. How could our whole world be turned topsy-turvy in a moment? I walked down her front path, looking at the first flowers springing up out of the ground, the sign of new life stirring in the soil. I thought, "How unfair." She who loved Spring, the tulips and daffodils, the azaleas in their fragrant and colorful glory, would never see this again. I lifted my face towards the sky and cried out, "Oh, God, please let her see Spring one last time."

It was the first day of Summer now, and we knew that there was not much time left. Mom couldn't eat. Her lips were parched and cracked. She could barely swallow water. I arrived at her house early that morning. I wanted to be with her. The past three months seemed a lifetime. The woman who gave birth to me now lay dying. She had wiped away my childhood tears, sent corny notes and boxes of red-hot candies to cheer me through college finals, and given me her wedding dress to wear. This woman sat up all night, two nights in a row, to encourage me through my first labor. I watched her now, this woman I loved, suffer through pain so deep that the strongest medicine barely touched it. Every day I cried and asked that she be released from this torture. Yet, every day I cried and asked for one more day to be with her and whisper how much I loved her.

"I love . . . " was all she could gasp between breaths. Even that cost more energy than she had. I sat next to her bed and held her hand, worn and callused from raising five children. The hand I was too embarrassed to hold in front of my friend that day so long ago as Mom walked us across the street. (Do you know,

Mom, how sorry I am that I felt that way?) The hand, cold and turning blue, that I now clung to, never wanting to let go.

Yes, the last three months seemed a lifetime, but also a blink of an eye. Enough time to say all I wanted to say, yet not enough to tell Mom how much I enjoyed being her friend these last few years, while sharing the common bond of motherhood. Who else would share my awe at my children's miracles—the first smile, the first word, the first step? The first "I wuv you." Who else would laugh so deeply over my daughter pouring the Cheerios into the baby pool because she had always wanted to swim in a bowl of cereal? Who else would love my children the way their mother's mother did?

"I love you, too," I said. I bent close to Mother's ear and prayed softly that her pain would lessen. That mine would also. That I could bear up under this. That she would be at peace in her heart and I in mine. Her breathing was labored. She couldn't move her head. Not even her eyes. But as I whispered of the love of God in her ear, I saw a tear roll down her cheek. Then another one. Even in her dying, my sorrow touched her mother's heart and she spoke back to me the only way she could.

A tear. It doesn't sound like much, does it? We've all cried. With a house full of children it seems we have tears around here every day. What with scraped knees, bee stings and various childhood traumas, big and small, it's tough to go a day without teary eyes and wet cheeks. But these tears were something else. A precious gift to me. How I wish I could have them in a bottle to hold. Maybe someday in Heaven I will.

I said my final "I love you," gently closed her eyelids, walked out the door and down the front path. As I passed, I looked down through my tears at the remains of the Spring flowers, dead or dying now. Their glorious display wilted and brown. I lifted my face towards the sky and remembered how I had asked that she who loved Spring would see this last one. And through my grief, the thought of the love of the Father in answering my plea, was a balm to my wounded heart. She had seen it all. Today was the first day of Summer.

—Elaine Munyan

Widow's Window

I sat at the kitchen table, absorbing the snowy morning through the window and adding it to my already melancholy spirit.

Window-watching had been my husband's ritual—not mine. But after Earl died I felt compelled to station myself at his favorite spot and monitor the world just as he had done during fifteen years of retirement. Most of the time, like this morning, I sipped tea and wondered why Earl enjoyed it so much. The scene from the window was always the same: a ridge of trees, a good-sized pond, Taylor's barn, a maze of fences, and a stretch of road winding somewhere.

I sighed and gently rubbed swollen fingers and aching hands. A touch of pity for my age and arthritis seemed appropriate on this gloomy winter day.

Not long ago there was no time to sit at a window and sip tea. How could life change so quickly? Even after Earl had retired, I remained busy. If I wasn't entertaining grandchildren or going to church, I was fishing with Earl at the pond or helping him in the garden. I was always preparing meals and clearing dishes from this oval table.

The lights in the kitchen flickered. I pulled my wool sweater close and shivered as a blast of cold air shook the window pane.

"If only the kids didn't live across town. If only I felt stronger!" Each thought depressed me more. I was practically a shut-in! There might as well be bars on this window!

At noon the sky was lighter. The road was unrecognizable to me but not, I hoped, for the driver of a truck bravely nibbling a path in my direction. The yellow headlights disappeared, then reappeared several times before I recognized Kirby Taylor's old blue truck inching its way to my drive.

"Why in the world would he be coming to visit on such a terrible day?" The question was soon answered. My neighbor stomped snow from his boots as I held open the door.

"What in the world have you got there?" I laughed.

Kirby Taylor carried in a life-sized, shivering bundle with tennis shoes.

"I hope you don't mind this intrusion, Dorothy," Taylor puffed. "My grandson is staying with me this week. I offered to keep Casey until the new baby arrived. Should be anytime now!"

I smiled at the wind-burned, young face with blond tousled hair peeking around the edges of a stocking cap.

"How wonderful, Casey!" I exclaimed. "Which do you prefer, a brother or a sister?"

Casey grinned and answered me with a quick exit behind his grandfather's jeans.

"He's a bit shy, Dorothy. We were getting along great until this snowstorm. My electricity went out this morning and the farmhouse is getting too chilly for a three-year-old."

"I'm glad you came over," I interrupted to say. "Casey, I'll bet you'd like some of Miss Dorothy's hot chocolate to drink."

Seconds later Casey was munching cookies and gulping hot chocolate at the oval table. My hands didn't bother me a bit as I dashed about the kitchen preparing Kirby's coffee and my tea. Kirby Taylor sat down at Earl's old place by the window and looked outside.

While Casey napped on a couch in the living room, Kirby talked about his friendship with Earl. Earl and I had welcomed Kirby Taylor three years earlier, when he moved to the neighboring farm after a city car accident killed his wife.

That was the reason Kirby had been so kind to me when Earl passed away last summer. He knew what I was going through. It was Kirby who notified the pastor when I couldn't get to church on my own anymore. Kirby had offered to take me to church once or twice, but I haven't taken him up on it—yet.

"I remember when Earl saved my cow," Kirby was saying. "He saw it caught in a barbed fence. If Earl hadn't been watching from this window at the time—" Kirby shrugged and shook his head. "Well, I wouldn't have that cow now."

The story jogged my memory of a similar incident. "Do you remember the mallard caught in the ice?"

"Oh, yes," he answered. "Earl noticed the duck in trouble and called me. We met at the pond. Had to chip away the ice from its wing to set it free."

Suddenly I realized that my husband's window watching had been considerably more than lazy entertainment.

The sky darkened and Kirby asked to use my phone to notify his son and daughter-in-law of his situation. Then he decided to return to his farm and check on things. I happily volunteered to keep Casey for as long as needed. We decided to use the windows of our houses as "lighthouses." If mine went out Kirby would immediately return. If his lights came on, then he would not be long in returning for Casey.

"I haven't the slightest idea what I'm going to do to entertain a three-year-old," I confided to my daughter over the phone after dinner. "I have no television, no pets, not even a piano for him to bang on!"

The problem was solved when Casey yelled for me to come to the window. "Look, Miss Dorothy," he squealed. "See the pretty circle in the sky!" I sat with Casey on my lap and we pretended the window was magic. The back yard became moors and mountains. We discovered a patch of snowflowers. His Grandpa's barn in the distance became a stable for the most unusual pets of Casey's choosing.

I silently prayed. "Thank you God, for this window. Forgive my self-pity. Help me to share the beauty as well as the blessings from Earl's window."

—Glenda Smithers

An Autumn Memory

I was ten-years-old. It was noon and I was going home from school for lunch. As I walked down the sidewalk toward my home, the autumn leaves fell and crunched beneath my footsteps. The leaves were brilliant in their many shades of gold, crimson, and brown. As I got closer to home, I saw my mother in the yard raking leaves. She saw me coming and smiled. When I walked into the yard, she told me my lunch was on the table. I went in and ate, and was soon on my way back to school.

I have believed all the years since that October, 1950, day that that memory was a gift from God. Just a few days after that autumn day, my mother died.

It has been many years now. My own children are grown and I am a grandmother. Seasons change, lives change. But each year when autumn leaves turn to vibrant hues and begin to fall, I am again ten years old. I am walking home from school. My mother sees me. She loves me.

—**Eunice Ann Badgley**

The Dream

I was born when my brother, Johnnie, was 15-years-old. I grew up under his loving, big-brother care. He took me for walks in the woods, sat me on his lap and combed my long hair, and took me to events such as car races, movies, and live musical shows that passed through town. He accompanied me to church and encouraged me to sing in the choir. He attended all of my school plays, recitals, and other functions. When I misbehaved, he was the buffer between Mother's anger and my deserved punishment.

Johnnie was interested in life and all it offered. He took a correspondence course and received his diploma. He took flying lessons and got his pilot's license. He collected muzzle-loading shotguns, taught himself to play the banjo and piano and performed for local dances.

Eventually, he married and fathered three children, but the bond between us was never broken. I still turned to him for advice. And as I grew older, he depended on me to be there for him when he had problems he was unable to solve.

Suddenly, when he was 39-years-old, he was stricken with a debilitating, fatal kidney disease. There were no dialysis machines then and no kidney transplants.

He was hospitalized and his wife, my sister, and I working in shifts, gave him 24-hour nursing care. During the six weeks he was in the hospital he was never alone. And then one rainy, April afternoon in 1954, he died.

My heart was broken. I had never experienced the death of a loved one and I was unable to cope. The family couldn't help me because they were suffering uncontrollable grief, too. Nearly every day I visited his grave site, and as I cried I asked him why he had left me. I felt I couldn't go on. Life had no meaning. Why was someone as decent and kind as Johnnie taken so early?

One night, two weeks later, I had a dream. *The doorbell was ringing and I walked down the steps and opened the front door.*

Standing at the bottom of the porch steps was Johnnie. He looked so well and his face beamed with joy. He was dressed in his brown suit, and his starched white collar glistened in the moonlight. His curly blond hair was neatly combed and his smile revealed the little gap between his front teeth. I was ecstatic! I stepped out onto the porch and started down the steps. He stepped back and said, "No. You can't touch me. I came back to tell you that I'm fine. I'm happy. And I want you to get on with your life."

I was overcome with joy and, ignoring his warning, I again started down the steps. And then I felt a hand on each of my shoulders holding me back. When I looked down I saw they were skeleton hands. I wasn't frightened. I simply knew that they were only a symbol of the death that separated us.

He smiled, then turned away and walked down the sidewalk. When he reached the end of the walk, he turned to face me and waved good-bye.

Since that night I have never dreamed of Johnnie again. In the years that followed, I have lost other loved ones but I have never experienced a dream about their passing. And although my dreams are forgotten by morning, this dream of Johnnie is as vivid forty years later as it was that night in May of 1954.

I went on with my life. I married and had three wonderful children. And my only regret is that they never had the opportunity to know what a compassionate uncle they had. But I am thankful that he was there to guide me through my growing-up years and I am certain that one day he will be there to welcome me "home."

—Lois Erisey Poole

Memories That Build The Future

Christmas heralded the most wondrous of celebrations within our close family of four married children and eight grandchildren. My husband and I owned a Bed & Breakfast which was also our home with five guest rooms in the mountain resort community of Lake Arrowhead, California. In our twelve years there, following retirement from corporate life, we closed the inn each December 24-27, making family a priority, and putting the rest of the world on hold.

On Christmas day everyone would merrily bustle in after stomping the snow from their feet. They came laden with gifts, favorite foods, and luggage to spend the night or as long as their time allowed. The house sparkled with the creativity of Christmas and flowed with love and laughter. True to tradition, a sea of balloons covered the English floral carpet, while a "Happy Birthday Jesus" banner, streamers and more balloons embellished the beams.

Then one April, the husband who had blown up the balloons and made the banners, the father and *Boompa* who had led the family in prayer and been in the middle of the games, went to be with Jesus.

Suddenly the rest of our lives—every family holiday, and especially Christmas, was changed forever. The great, lovable European-style Bed & Breakfast was quickly sold. I had no heart to do this without him.

Every Christmas in our mountain home had been a treasured memory-maker. But the one which unknowingly became our last one there, seemed sweeter, more tender, more meaningful and precious than all the others. We recognized it then, but even more so later, as a special gift from God! Throughout the first year of our loss, we often reflected upon our cherished last Christmas, and prayed for strength to face the next one without my husband.

Another Christmas came. And yes, we had balloons, and the "Jesus is the Reason for the Season" banner, Jesus' birthday cake, stories, and singing by the piano. Love and beauty abounded in every sense in a different setting. We still ate too much turkey dinner, laughed and hugged. Yet the eyes of our hearts observed each others' emotions quivering just below the surface to make it through the day.

But in the midst of our loss, we knew that we forever had what some families never had—precious, joyous memories, traditions we will prayerfully pass on for future generations to cherish and further embellish to preserve and make their own. We find comfort that our separation from our loved one is only temporary. We will be together again for eternity.

Even so, while here on earth, my heart weeps each Christmas. Glistening through tear-filled eyes, the exquisite glory of God's gift through Christ's birth gives me a peace that only the Lord can give to the brokenhearted.

—Lila Peiffer

Crossing The River Called Grief

It had been fifteen months since Steve was diagnosed with acute leukemia. Many friends and family stood around his bed, watching and praying, as Steve, my husband, friend and the love of my life took his last breath. It was the saddest day of my life.

After the nurses removed all the tubes and machines, Steve's wedding ring was placed into my hand. Walking toward Steve's room, my heart raced in anticipation of seeing him. He lay on the bed, lifeless. I sat beside him in a chair and felt so alone, realizing at that moment that I was no longer a wife . . . I was now a widow. Sitting there, the thought came to me, "It's just you and me, Lord."

As our children entered the room, I left them and went back to the waiting room. A nurse approached and said, "Mrs. Bagne, where do you want the remains to be sent?" Did she say "remains?" This was only the beginning; so much was still ahead.

Two days later I looked at Steve lying in a casket. He wore his church clothes and his eyes were closed as if he were resting. It was as if at any moment he would wake up. But Steve wasn't there! It was just the body I used to live with and love. How on earth am I supposed to leave the viewing room and go on living?

Some time later, a social worker described grief as a river that takes a long journey. No one could cross this river for me. They may walk with me, encourage me, or stand on the other side and call to me. But the journey is mine and life is on the other side. I never forgot her words. They would come to mind often in the weeks and months ahead.

But initially, I thought it would be different—God had something else in mind *for me*. I stepped off the bank . . . in a hurry to get to the other side. The Bible says that sorrow endures for a night, but joy comes in the morning. Little did I know the night would be long and the morning would be years away.

There are many stones in this river called grief. Some are

quickly passed over and some are to rest upon. As I stepped off that bank of numbness, I planted my foot firmly on the stone of pain. I thought my heart would literally burst from the ache inside. I would lie in bed at night and cry for Steve, not for God. God could not be trusted. After all, He had let this happen to me when He could have stopped it.

Now I was on the stone called anger and I lingered there for quite awhile. People tried to offer comfort with pat answers like, "He's not in pain anymore," "You're young. You'll get over it." But I was *never* going to get over this! Some people were helpful, though, as they listened and didn't try to take away my pain, even when I blamed God.

I left the stone of anger for awhile, leaping to the stone of depression. During my stay there I could not sleep or concentrate. I was very forgetful and tired all the time. All normal living was absurd.

As I traveled back and forth among the stones of pain, anger, and depression, I became very tired of this part of the river called grief. However, I was never allowed to return to the bank of numbness.

Then the stone of guilt was in my way. All the "what ifs" and "should haves" came flooding in. *What if* we had gone to the hospital sooner. *I should have* been kinder to him. I was tormented by these thoughts and at the same time afraid to tell anyone about them. They might confirm them as true. It was about this time that I began to speak to God again. This guilt drove me to Him, because somehow I knew the burden of this was too great to carry alone. In His faithfulness He brought relief.

I have traveled the river called grief for over two years now; in many ways it has become my friend. We understand each other a little better. Recently, I've touched my toe on the stone of adjustment. This stone is one I never wanted to place my foot upon. It didn't seem right that I would ever adjust to life without Steve. It was like being unfaithful somehow. But there is no life in the middle of the river, only on the other side. Everyone has their own timetable for crossing the river. I know I will never "get over" losing Steve, but I will adjust to Steve's being gone. I've made many return-crossings of the river, but it has become easier to move about without being pulled under.

As I stand on the stone of adjustment, I can see the bank of recovery. Being able to look back, seeing how far I have come and knowing life is ahead, drives me on. My legs are a bit wobbly from the long trip, but, in spite of the blow it took, my heart is still beating. My faith is stronger, though challenged, and I actually believe there may be a future after all.

—Gwen Bagne

Saying Good-bye

The dreaded phone call came at 2 a.m. Dad had another heart attack! He had been taken to the nearest hospital . . . he was dying! I had gone through this same experience three months earlier, and knew exactly what to do. I began to pray and ask God to save Dad's life, once again.

My father had been forced into early retirement at age 60 because of a series of heart attacks. Today, surgeons could perform bypass surgery and prolong his life; but twenty years ago the procedure wasn't available.

Dad had worked since he was eleven years old, and wasn't sure how to handle retirement. But, soon he developed a number of hobbies and learned to enjoy his new life of leisure.

Then, on June 6, 1980, I received the first phone call telling me that Dad had been rushed to the hospital. His heart had stopped twice and he wasn't expected to live through the night.

Prayer has always been a major part of my life. So, after I hung up and before I drove to the hospital, I prayed, "Oh, Lord, please allow Dad to live. He's so vital to our family, I can't picture life without him."

God's message came through loud and clear, "Have faith! Your father will live! Regardless of what you see or hear, believe that he will live!"

Suddenly, the most incredible sense of peace flowed through me! Isaiah 26:3 came to mind: *Thou doest keep him in perfect peace whose mind is stayed on thee.*

I arrived at the hospital and joyfully shared God's promise with everyone who would listen. My family and the hospital staff thought I was in shock and denial. They could see that Dad was in his death throes, but I kept assuring them that he would survive.

As family and friends huddled in the sterile waiting room, the cardiologist gave periodic updates. At one point, he gravely announced, "Mr. Purcell's heart is so severely damaged, only the stem is still beating . . . it won't be long now." Panic filled my mother's eyes, and my sisters began to weep. But, I reminded them to have faith, pray, and keep their eyes on God. His promise wouldn't fail!

By the next morning, the news spread throughout the hospital . . . a miracle had occurred! Dad's heart stem was beating strongly, and, against all odds, it appeared he was going to live!

Three weeks later, "the miracle man" went home to recuperate.

And so, in the early morning hours of September 26, 1980, when I heard that Dad was, once again, fighting for his life, I promptly prayed for another miracle. However, God's message, this time, was different. "Your father is coming Home, now. You've said your good-byes."

I thought about the previous three months and realized that it was the most rewarding, quality time my family had ever spent together. It suddenly dawned on me that we had been tying up loose ends, saying and doing the things we'd never said and done, before.

We had spent those three months saying good-bye.

Then an overwhelming grief hit me. But, God reminded me of Isaiah 26:3, and, once again, I was filled with His perfect peace . . . a peace that lasted throughout the trying days ahead, and well beyond.

—Ruth E. McDaniel

4

Making Difficult Decisions

For God did not give us a spirit of timidity, but a spirit of power, of love and of self-discipline.

II Timothy 1:7

A Purpose In It All

Jan Phipps glanced out the airplane window as it taxied down the runway. The sky looked as if the spirit had been sucked out of it, leaving nothing but a steely-gray void. Her heart and body felt the same.

Having just gone through a series of grueling tests at a clinic near her home, Jan wasn't ready to repeat the process. The hospital's laboratory staff had discovered she had chronic lymphocytic leukemia, and her doctor wanted her to go to the Mayo Clinic in Rochester, Minnesota, for a second opinion. He phoned for an appointment, explaining the seriousness of Jan's condition.

Jan didn't want to go. "You'll be gone only four days," her doctor reminded her.

She looked at her husband Cal. He nodded his agreement.

"Then I'll go alone," Jan said. "You're needed here."

Her only sister Mary was terminally ill with lung cancer. Cal would be a comfort to her and her family as well as Mary and Jan's 79-year-old mother.

Dear God, Jan thought, as she said good-bye, *I may never see Mary again in this world.*

Packing and boarding the plane that March morning had stripped Jan of her strength. She leaned back in the seat and tried to relax. But pain from her spastic colon jabbed her and she clutched her side.

Reaching into her purse for a pain pill, Jan glimpsed her reflection in the mirror on the flap. She barely recognized herself. Her jaws puffed out as if she had the mumps. The puffiness was caused by the swollen parotid glands in front of her ears.

Jan felt awful. Tossing the pill into her mouth, she swallowed hard and closed her eyes. *I simply can't go through those horrible medical tests again. When I reach Kansas City, I'll get off the plane and take a return flight home.*

In an attempt to get comfortable, Jan turned toward the

window, eyes still closed. Suddenly, a brightness warmed her face. She opened her eyes and looked out the window.

A silvery, bright sunbeam had burst through the overcast sky. It was shining directly on Jan. *Every cloud has a silver lining*, she thought, *but not my clouds*.

Then she heard an inner voice clearly say, "Jan, don't turn back. I have a purpose for you. Prepare yourself. Trust Me."

At that moment she experienced a quiet, calming assurance. Though nothing else had changed, she knew she was in touch with God—the source of power who would see her through anything.

Jan recalled the words from her Bible: *Though I walk in the midst of trouble, Thou wilt revive me . . .* (Psalm 138:7). The silvery sunbeam had given her hope. She would continue on to Minnesota!

When Jan checked into Mayo Clinic the staff gave her priority treatment. Blood tests began that very afternoon. But, after four days of tests, charts, computer print-outs, and instructions as to what to do and where to go next, the end of the procedure was still nowhere in sight. Jan desperately wanted to go home, but God had said, "Don't turn back." She clung to the memory of His voice.

"Father, I'm so weak," she prayed continuously, "Give me the strength and courage I need to go on."

And He did.

On the ninth day the results of the final test were computed and Jan's doctor gave her the report. "Well, Mrs. Phipps," he said, "You certainly have caused an uproar. Over the years we've had three million patients go through this clinic. You are only the sixth person to have gamma heavy chain disease and prolific protein in your hemoglobin."

"What does that mean?" Jan asked in horror.

"You do have leukemia—an extremely rare type. As far as we know, only twelve persons in the world have it." He then asked if she would consider staying and allowing the immunology lab to take a unit of plasma and a 24-hour collection of urine from her. This would be used in search of a serum for a variety of diseases, including cancer.

"You don't have to give me your answer today," he added.

Already she was worn out and Cal had phoned to say that Mary was slipping fast. *Should I try to get home as quickly as possible? I still might arrive in time to see Mary once more.* But no, she couldn't leave. God had said He wanted her here. She was sure this was the purpose He had for her.

"Yes, doctor," Jan cried, "begin now!" Inside, a huge sob shook her body and she cried for a long time.

The next day arrangements were made with the Clinic's Advanced Blood Laboratory for further tests and collections. The technician explained that these collections would be made every few months by her doctor back home and mailed to the Mayo Clinic.

On April 1, Jan's thirteenth day in Rochester, a clinic employee helped her board a plane bound for home. Eight days later Mary died.

After Mary's services, Jan lay on her bed to rest. *I missed being with Mary during more of her final days,* she thought, *but I'm thankful I had a small part in the discovery of a future cure for cancer.*

She fluffed up her pillow and turned onto her side. Sunbeams bursting through clouds would always remind her of Psalm 138, that even in the midst of trouble God would revive her. Because He had.

—Doris C. Crandall

This Is A Test

Because I live thirty miles west of Chicago I leave home early in the morning to "beat the traffic." One of the things I love to do on that drive is to worship God, with the help of cassette tapes and the radio. I'll never forget the morning I was listening to the Brooklyn Tabernacle Choir. One hundred and eighty voices, saved off the streets of Brooklyn, singing like they meant it, with energy and power, were lifting me before the Lord as I sang and worshipped. As I approached the city, the sun was rising behind the cityscape. Through the morning haze, rays of beautiful orange cast their shafts between the buildings. My heart thought, *What a glorious Creator we have.* I was in ecstasy!

Pulling up to a stoplight, I noticed a taxicab facing me with his left blinker on and his wheel cranked to the left. He kept inching forward. I knew what he had in his heart. *He wants to cut me off when the light turns green!* And so, right in the midst of my worship, God said, "We interrupt the normal programming for this test." Because I was in such close fellowship with God at that moment you would think that I would let the taxicab by, since it's important to be understanding and loving. After all, maybe the taxi driver was late for breakfast and his wife was waiting for him. Maybe he had just got a call from a woman in labor. Whatever—here was my opportunity to reveal the true nature of my worship.

The light turned green, and I "nailed" the accelerator. The taxi driver nailed his, too, and he just missed me as I went flying by. He was making a U-turn, and we ended up at the next light next to each other. We Christians have such a limited set of gestures to use. All I could do was to look at him, throw my hands up and say, "What are you doing?" The light turned green, and I drove on. But when I walked through those legacy-laden arches at Moody (Moody Bible Institute), the Spirit said, "Stowell, we got a good look at you this morning. There's something to work on in your life!"

What good is trouble? Among other things, it reveals where I am in the growth process in terms of my conformity to the image and character of Christ. . .

—Joseph M. Stowell

The Apron Strings

One of the most difficult times for me as a mother was allowing my oldest son to go away to college. When he graduated from high school, I wrote him the following letter:

Dear Rich,

Today is your high school graduation. I have spent the last eighteen years teaching and guiding you. Now it is time to let you go and to allow you to choose your own way.

As you were growing up, I shared your victories and defeats. I cheered at your swim meets and applauded at your cello concerts. I watched a skinny, freckle-faced blonde boy change into a handsome, six-foot-three muscular young man.

As a mother, the hardest job for me is to let go—to allow our roles to change. I worked hard at being your mother, and now I want to enjoy being your friend. As a token of my feelings and my confidence in you, I'm enclosing my apron strings in this letter. They are cut off from my apron to symbolize your total freedom.

Yet, you know that I will be only a phone call away. I want to continue to share your life, to hear about your experiences, to be there when you need me. The difference is that now you are in the driver's seat, and I'm the passenger.

I believe in you, and I love you very much.

Congratulations, Son!

All my love,

MOM

As parents, we spend many years helping our children establish firm foundations for their lives. As they grow older, we hope they will continue to build on those foundations. Finally, the time comes to hand them the hammers and nails and let them go. In this way, we allow them to lead their own lives, make their own decisions, and accept the responsibility for their own mistakes.

At the time of Rich's graduation, problems in my own life

made it especially difficult for me to cut my apron strings. My husband and I had talked seriously about obtaining a legal separation. Because of my loneliness and overwhelming needs, I found myself clinging to my children even though I realized it was wrong. There is a delicate balance between maintaining a close family atmosphere and smothering our grown children.

I look back to the day ten years ago when I wrote that letter to a high school graduate. I compare that with the relationship I now have with my twenty-eight-year-old son. He truly is one of my best friends. Although his present job takes him around the world, he continues to keep in touch by telephone and E-mail.

Today, no matter how many miles separate me from my firstborn, we will always be close. When he returns home for a visit, I share his adventures and his dreams as I always have and hope I always will.

—Susan Titus Osborn

To Be A Woman

While showering one morning in June of 1976, I discovered a small lump in my right breast. Later that day, Dr. Baker tried to be optimistic as he examined me and then scheduled surgery for the next morning.

That night my husband kept the conversation on a cheerful note, but when visiting hours were over, his kiss was long and lingering. Joe was an exceptionally handsome man. More than once I'd seen women turn to appreciate his good looks. If a mastectomy were necessary, would he find me repulsive?

The next afternoon I awakened in the recovery room. Through the haze of anesthesia, I saw the intravenous bottle attached to my left arm, felt a dull pressure under the mountainous bandage on my right side, and knew the worst had happened. I regained consciousness again back in my room and whispered to Joe, "I'm sorry." Tears filled his eyes and he gently patted my hand.

That night, before I drifted off to sleep, I poured out all my fears and pain to my Heavenly Father. The old familiar, "Please, God, help me," somehow didn't seem positive enough so I changed it to "Thank you, God, for healing me." Suddenly, I sensed a miraculous difference in my attitude. That positive affirmation strengthened me to begin acting as though I were healed. I used my right arm as I walked down the halls.

Triumph over my emotions was short-lived, however. Three days later Dr. Baker helped me into my robe and escorted me to the staff lounge where we could talk privately. "The cancer had metastasized from the breast to the lymph glands," he explained. "There's another problem, too. Pathology found a second type of cancer, lobular carcinoma, which is deadly because it gives no early warning signs of its presence. I recommend we take a random sampling of tissue from your remaining breast to determine if the cancer is there also, but you have twenty-four hours to decide."

Shattered, I returned to my room, pulled the privacy curtain around my bed, and lay in a cocoon of despair too numb even to cry. Where my solitary thoughts would have led isn't hard to guess, but unexpectedly a warm hand clasped mine. It was the chaplain making his rounds. He said, "At best life can only be lived by the day, but when a person is facing serious illness, life should be lived by the hours or even minutes. Too often, I've seen people waste their final days in the grip of self pity and recriminations, leaving their loved ones with unpleasant memories." His words wrapped me in God's strength. Then he anointed my forehead with oil and prayerfully placed me in Jesus' gentle hands.

When the chaplain left, he opened the privacy curtain and the afternoon sun was streaming into the room spotlighting the beautiful bouquet Joe had sent the day of surgery. It was a large pyramid-shaped arrangement of golden mums and greenery with a regal bird-of-paradise bloom at each triangle point. So eye-catching were those blooms that people passing in the hall stopped to admire them. That morning, those regal blooms had wilted so the cleaning woman had deftly plucked them from the arrangement and threw them away. Still the bouquet endured, its beauty undiminished.

As I studied the bouquet, an almost mystical thought came to me. I could visualize the loving hands that created it—choosing first the long-lasting mums, arranging them carefully in a pleasing shape, then as a final touch adding those dramatic bird of-paradise. Hadn't I, too, been created in just that way? After all, these eye-catching symbols of womanhood had been added at puberty. If they were gone, wouldn't I, like my bouquet, still be attractive? Isn't femininity spiritual as well as physical?

And so my decision was made. I would not allow a biopsy, but would insist on another mastectomy. Random samples of tissue might miss something; cancer could appear later without warning signals. Dr. Baker applauded my decision and sent me home until surgery was performed eight days later. The resultant lab work disclosed two microscopic cells that might have been overlooked in a hit-and-miss technique.

Traumatic? Yes. It wasn't comforting to have doctors speak in terms of remission rather than cure. But I tried to remember that each of us is following our own special destiny, and I bowed to those plans.

Today, twenty years later, I'm not handicapped physically or emotionally, and I'm much stronger spiritually. My femininity is securely in place.

—**Betty Huff**

A Cupboard Full Of Memories

"As soon as they learn to walk, they begin to walk away," someone said. Whoever made that statement knew what parenthood is all about—raising our children to finally walk out of our lives.

For years we prepared ourselves and our son, Jim, for this moment: the day he would leave home in pursuit of a life of his own. I thought I was ready.

My husband and I tried to make his transition as easy as possible. In an effort to help him get started on his new road of independence, we searched the house for items we thought he could use.

Rummaging through the house became a journey back in time. An old couch, the kitchen set we had used since Jim was two years old, a few tray tables and a smorgasbord of odd glasses and old dishes were all set aside for him to take.

Out of all the items we gathered, however, none were as nostalgic as our hodgepodge of worn-out plates and glasses from days gone by. Jelly jars converted into drinking glasses, outdated Ronald McDonald plates and the Big-Gulp refillable glasses we never refilled were among our family treasures packed and ready to go. With them went our everyday dishes—the dishes with chipped off edges and faded designs which we had used each day for more years than I can remember.

All were special, since they represented a precious time in our lives. They were a tangible reminder of the times our family prayed together, shared together, cried together and laughed together—a time that was about to come to an end.

Tearfully, I sat on a nearby chair savoring the moment as if to recapture a glimpse of the past. Reluctantly, I continued to fill each box, realizing that one important chapter of our lives had come to a close and I had to let go.

My son left home with a box of careworn, invaluable cups and plates under his arm, ready to embark on life's next adventure. As I watched him walk away, I thought about the little boy who sat at the kitchen counter dunking cookies in milk while finishing the picture that would soon grace my refrigerator door. Reflections of a simpler life held my imagination captive. I smiled through my tears as I thought about his childhood innocence.

Heavy-hearted, I returned to my work, replacing the old dishes with the new. Somehow it wasn't the same.

I gazed upon the neatly-stacked plates, uniform bowls and matching glasses positioned where the old ones once were. I protested, "But life isn't like that, Lord—all perfect and neatly stacked." Inwardly, I longed for the days of mismatched glasses, scribbled artwork, sticky hands and bruised knees.

Then something happened. The Lord gently spoke to my heart saying, "This isn't the end but a new beginning." As God's presence engulfed me, I knew that my life would again be filled with new memories to cherish.

Scripture says, *To everything there is a season, and a time to every purpose under the heaven . . .* (Ecclesiastes 3:1 KJV). One season had ended, making room for yet another. It was time for me to look ahead and not behind—to let go and trust God.

That meant loving Jim enough to allow him to walk on his own and chart his own course—trusting that the Christian principles we laid down for him throughout his childhood would stand. So that one day he, too, will build a cupboard full of memories overflowing with chipped plates and mismatched glasses.

—Tina Krause

Red And White Carnations

This was the first Mother's Day since Grandmother passed away. I dreaded going to church and seeing families sitting together with their moms. *I'm only sixteen. I shouldn't be sitting alone.* But my mother had abandoned us years earlier and my parents were divorced.

"Maybe, I should have stayed home," I said to myself as I walked up the church steps. A kind, elderly gentleman opened the large wooden door.

"Good morning, and Happy Mother's Day." Mrs. Spence greeted several churchgoers in the narthex. "Please take a red carnation if your mother is living, and a white one if she has passed on."

I must have stood in front of the large basket of flowers for several minutes. I couldn't decide which one to take.

"My *real* mother is alive, but dead to me," I reasoned. She left when I was two years old, and I'd only seen her twice.

The first time was two years earlier at my brother's high school graduation. Mrs. Davis, one of my teachers, came up to me and said, "Barbara, this is your mother."

"My mother!" I snapped. "What is she doing here?"

Behind Mrs. Davis stood a brown-haired, short lady with a warm smile.

"Hi, Barbara. You've turned out to be quite a young lady," she greeted me.

"Hello," I managed to respond. She looked at me and waited for me to say something else but I didn't know what to say or do. I just stood there and stared at her, wondering, *Do I look like her?*

Janice, one of my classmates, rescued me by asking me to meet some friends on the stage for a picture. I excused myself and made sure I got lost in the crowd.

The second time I saw her was at Grandmother's funeral. She

tried to talk to me, but I just looked down. I didn't feel like talking to anyone.

Which flower should I take? Grandmother Benedict was like a *real* mother to me. She took care of me, went shopping with me, and saw to it that I did my homework. I had fond memories of her sitting by her quilting frame, singing hymns in her native Hungarian tongue. I would sit and listen to how she immigrated to America, and how God provided for her needs. She would always say, "Use what God gives you wisely. If you pray for your daily bread, then don't waste it."

I knew she had influenced me in the same way she made patchwork quilts. Fragmented pieces, when sewn together, formed a complete pattern. The dominant pieces of our relationship were love, joined together by threads of laughter and tears.

I concluded, "I really should take a white carnation." I pulled one from the basket and took a seat in the back pew. The organist began the prelude and a reverence settled over the congregation. I sat clutching the white carnation while my heart held tightly to the past. *Most of the people here know that my real mother is alive. Do they understand why I took a white carnation? Does God understand that I'm hurting?*

The choir began to take their seats and the organist played softly. I raised my eyes and focused on the large wooden cross behind the choir loft.

"Oh, Jesus, You do understand, don't You? You were hurt. You were rejected by those You loved. Yet, You chose to forgive them. Help me to do the same. If I meet my Mother again, help me to be loving. Thank You that you are always near and that You promise to never leave. Thank you for eternal life and that I'll see Grandmother again. Amen."

The organist continued to play as the pastor took his seat behind the pulpit. I looked back in the narthex and noticed the basket of flowers. I quickly, but quietly, walked back to the flower arrangement to put the white carnation back. I wanted to prove to God and myself, that I was willing to deal with the past, and the future.

All of the red carnations were taken, but my eye caught a glimpse of one single variegated red and white carnation lying on the table. It probably had been taken out of the basket because it was neither all red nor all white.

"God does understand my feelings," I whispered. "The florist didn't make a mistake. This carnation is just right for me on this Mother's Day. I do have a mother, who is alive and needs my forgiveness. Grandmother Benedict is gone for now, but alive spiritually, and in my memories."

I took the red and white carnation back to my seat, and entered into the worship service.

—Barbara Benedict Hibschman

The Letter

It was unusual for me to be home at 11:30 in the morning; even more unusual for the mailman to arrive so early. Life, it seemed, had been unusual for the past few weeks. I pondered my sense of emptiness and confusion as I strolled toward the mailbox.

After years of banging away in the corporate rat race, I had finally taken an impulsive plunge into my own business. From my husband Lewis' perspective, it appeared more like a suicidal jump into an empty swimming pool. Actually, he was quite angry and hurt that I would take action without his knowledge.

I moaned, *Why can't he emotionally support me? Is this why we're experiencing new struggles in our mid-life years?*

For almost ten years I had felt loved and supported. Lew was my best friend. We called ourselves "soul mates." Recently, though, I felt as if I were watching our relationship slowly disintegrate before my eyes.

Shortly after I announced my resignation, Lew left on an extended business trip. He had always traveled a lot, but this time he would be gone longer—twelve days. Before his departure, I was caught up in a whirlwind of activities as I developed the marketing materials for my new endeavor. I apologized profusely for overbooking my schedule and not being available to drive him to the airport. A quick hug and kiss—and he was gone. I rationalized, *These twelve days will be a great time to get all my work organized, then we can have some quality time.*

Lew had called me from his business trip sounding oddly detached. He expressed an emptiness about our relationship. "Where is it going?" he queried me.

What is he saying? I didn't know how to answer.

A week that should have passed quickly in all my busyness became a string of endless days and sleepless nights. I became obsessed with his comments. "Is it another woman, true discontentment, or are you simply falling out of love?" I questioned him. He expressed his love and commitment but somehow they seemed hollow.

Now a month had passed since Lew returned but the promised quality time had never appeared. I longed for him to become my best friend again. "All right, Lord," I prayed, "do surgery on my heart. My personal ambitions have become a wedge between us. Somehow make us soul mates once more."

A heaviness in my heart and spirit enveloped me as I reached the mailbox. The mailman had just left when I noticed the bundle of letters still sitting on top of our community mailbox. *Hmm . . . odd that he would drive off without them*, I thought. *These must be letters left for outgoing mail.* The one on top was some type of magazine order with Lew's distinct and perfect printing, The stack was bundled with a rubber band and too thick to stuff into the narrow slot.

I removed the band and inserted the first letter, the second, the third. My heart skipped a beat. The next letter looked like a greeting card in its soft lavender envelope. The precise printing again was easy to discern and it was addressed to a woman. My heart began to pound. I started to slip it into the outgoing mail slot. I really tried. I just could not let go of it. Hurriedly, I crammed in the other letters and removed my personal mail from our box. The lavender menace stayed stuck to my left hand,

Safely inside my front door, I collapsed on the stair case. *I have to know. I must be crazy. It's probably a thank you note to one of his business contacts. She's probably a grandmother! If I open it and it's nothing, I'll have to tell him what a crazy fool I am. If I open it and it's something . . .* that thought stuck in my throat like a tennis ball.

"Let me be a crazy fool, Lord." I ripped open the letter. It was one of those wispy, sophisticated cards with a subtle message like, "I thought of you today and . . ." My heart crumbled to a million pieces in one split second and I hadn't yet read a single word. But the note that followed explained a lot of things.

For weeks God had been protecting me from the lies and deceit. In His perfect timing, God profoundly revealed the truth to me that spring day. His divine intervention exposed the truth that Lew so desperately needed to confess.

Before I went into my husband's office to dial his pager number, I fell into a heap and prayed, "Lord, only You know the truth. Only You how to put us back together again. I love You and I love my husband. I know I am capable of the same sin. I crossed that line in my first marriage and almost again with Lew."

With His fullness of grace, God gave me a spirit of complete forgiveness. In that moment of betrayal and pain, His love poured within me mercy and compassion. I remembered the Psalm, *A broken spirit and a contrite heart, he will not despise.*

The ringing phone jolted me into the present. "Lewis, I read a letter today . . . I shouldn't have opened your mail but I just had to. I love you. I forgive you. Please. Come home." He did and we began a long journey of restoration.

That was three years ago. As Lew and I walked along the beach holding hands recently, I shared how the Lord had helped me through those first painful months. Every time I would start to feel anxious about our marriage and the future, God would remind me of His careful intervention in the mailman leaving a bundle of letters on top of a mailbox. I could trust such a God who is capable of far more than I could ever ask or imagine.

—Danna Demetre

Sustaining Life

My father should have been raised as a cowboy on the open plains. Actually, he almost was. Born in 1900, he led a rough-rider life, trading with Indians in the Northwest and scaling the highest peaks of the Rockies. I loved following in his footsteps, riding fast horses, hiking high mountains, and camping under the moon and stars. Dad was my hero.

When I was little, he took my sisters and me to see a movie about Eskimos called *The Young Savages*. I was troubled by a scene in which an elderly Eskimo who was dying was left behind on an ice floe. We talked about it on the way home, and although I can't remember my father's words, I knew that Daddy would probably have chosen the same path.

I forgot about that movie until decades later when my father became physically and mentally debilitated by a series of strokes that left him virtually bedridden. It was the long-feared nightmare that we, while growing up, always pushed from our minds.

Our ninety-year-old dad was but a shadow of his former self. His withered boy frame couldn't hide the undaunted spirit that twinkled from his blue eyes. It crushed our hearts to think that Daddy was probably going to die within a year, maybe months, or even weeks.

The family house in Maryland was sold. Mother moved with Dad to Florida where he resided in a cheery, little nursing home. Mom walked from my uncle's house to the nursing home every morning to care for her husband's needs and then returned at night after he was put to bed. My sisters and I often visited and Linda, Jay, and Kathy most frequently stretched their visits so they could help our mother and dad.

Then, in a span of less than two weeks, everything changed. My father began to quickly fail. He was rushed to the hospital. An IV was inserted. The tube was later removed when his body bloated and lungs filled. He was sent back to the nursing home.

Our family collapsed in exhaustion. We agonized and conferred with doctors. After much prayer and painful discussion, we made a decision: no feeding tube. It was clear Daddy was dying, and knowing my father, he would not want the process of his dying prolonged. My sisters and mom tenderly cared for Daddy around the clock during his last days, camping on couch pillows by his bedside and giving him what little water he could take.

Within days I received a phone call from Jay. Daddy had passed away. I sat for a long moment and then put my thoughts on paper.

In that little nursing home, my mother had sat vigil with Dad for over a year and a-half, helping him daily and spreading the joy of the Lord to every elderly person up and down each hallway. In this last week, I joined my sisters and Mom there. it was obvious Dad was failing fast.

I had to leave after a few days—it was a tearful departure, knowing I'd never see my father again this side of eternity. But now, just days later, they called to say how Dad had turned to my mother, opened both his blue eyes for the first time in days, gave her a big, full smile and languished for a moment in what they emphatically described as a "glow." It must have been the glow of God's presence because then . . . he passed away.

My mother, sisters, a recreational therapist, and a nurse held hands around his bed and sang a doxology. From there, my sisters canvassed the hallways telling people, "Daddy just went to heaven to be with the Lord . . . isn't that exciting?"

—Joni Eareckson Tada

Good-bye Again

Mother stood waiting outside the doorway.

The suitcases were packed and standing in the hallway, ready to be loaded into the car. We children ran around the driveway, laughing and playing while we waited for Daddy. Suddenly his tall, handsome figure appeared in the doorway, overcoat slung over one arm, hat on his head. We ran to him, dreading what we knew would be another long separation. He took each of us in his strong arms, held us tightly, and then kissed us good-bye.

I couldn't bear to look into his eyes, because I knew they would be glistening with tears. Though there were many such good-byes while we were growing up, it never got easier. We backed away and watched as Daddy took mother in his arms, kissing her warmly and firmly, knowing it would be some time before he would hold her again.

Then, before we knew it, Daddy was whisked away in the car, around the curves and down the steep mountain drive. We listened to the retreating sound of the engine and waited for the final "toot" of the horn as he reached the gate. Another plane to catch, another city, another crusade, another period of weeks before we would be together as a family once more.

I turned to look at Mother, sensing her feeling of loss and loneliness. Her eyes were bright with unshed tears, but there was a beautiful smile on her face as she said, "Okay, let's clean the attic! Then we'll have LaoNaing and Lao I up for supper!" (Chinese for maternal grandmother and maternal grandfather. Mother's parents, the Nelson Bells, served for twenty-five years as missionaries to China. They retired to a home only a mile down the mountain from us.)

Not once did my mother ever make us feel that by staying behind she was sacrificing her life for us children. By her sweet, positive example, her consistently unselfish spirit, and her total reliance upon the person of Jesus Christ, we were kept from

bitterness and resentment. We learned, instead, to look for ways
to keep busy and prepare for Daddy's homecoming.

Years later, I asked Mother how she had endured so many years
of good-byes. She laughed and quoted the old mountain man
who said, "Make the least of all that goes, and the most of all
that comes."

> We live a time
> secure;
> beloved and loving,
> sure
> it cannot last
> for long,
> then—
> the good-byes come
> again—again—
> like a small death,
> the closing of a door.
> One learns to live
> with pain.
> One looks ahead,
> not back—
> never back,
> only before.
> And joy will come again—
> warm and secure,
> if only for the now,
> laughing, we endure.

—Ruth Bell Graham

Mother's example returns to my heart again and again
through the years: Don't regret what is past. Cherish what you
have. Look forward to all that is to come. And most important
of all, rely moment by moment on Jesus Christ.

—Gigi Graham Tchividjian

It Wasn't About Kathleen After All

Kathleen. My stomach churned at the sound of her name. It followed me everywhere. Two Kathleens in a class I attended. The name of my friend's roommate. And the woman I worked with on a church committee had her eyes and short wavy hair.

I dreamt about her. I thought about her. I was obsessed with her—the woman who had disrupted my marriage, slept with my husband, and ultimately married him.

The rage, resentment, guilt, and anger I felt continued for months—years. I went into counseling. I attended classes. I read books on how to let go. I talked to other divorced women. I ran and hiked and slept and ate—to avoid my feelings. I drove for miles to nowhere. I screamed. I prayed.

I did everything I knew how to do—except surrender.

Then one Saturday morning I was drawn to a day-long seminar on forgiveness sponsored by the church I was attending at the time. The leader opened with discussion and examples of the meaning of forgiveness, and then he asked us to close our eyes and locate one person we needed to forgive and then to see if we would be *willing* to forgive.

My first thought, Kathleen, of course. That awful name sent my stomach churning again. I could hardly stay in my chair. I wanted to run out of the room. "God, how can I ever forgive such a woman?" I pleaded silently. "She ruined my life. I can't let her off."

But her name and her face persisted in my mind. Then I felt the Holy Spirit nudging me gently from within. "Would you be willing to release her? And to forgive yourself too?"

I went hot, then cold. My hands shook. My heart pounded so fast I thought it would burst. "All right, Lord, I'll try, but I can't do it by myself." The words barely escaped my lips when suddenly an incredible, profound shift took place within me. I can't explain it. I simply—let go of Kathleen, just like that. For the first time in my life I surrendered to the Holy Spirit, allowing Him to do within me what I could not do for myself—what I had doggedly resisted for years.

Within seconds, energy coursed through every cell of my body. My mind became alert, my heart lightened. I saw everything in a brand new way. It was suddenly clear to me that as long as I hold judgment against even one person—deserved or not—I separate myself from God. How self-righteous I had been. How important it had been for me to be right.

The following Monday, I walked into my office and wrote Kathleen a letter. I felt the power of the Holy Spirit guiding my fingers at the keyboard. The words spilled out of me. I told her how I had judged her and hated her all those years—but then on Saturday, finally, I had released her. I apologized for every cruel thought I had held against her. I signed my name and mailed the letter that afternoon.

On Wednesday morning the phone rang. There was no mistaking the voice on the other end of the line. "Karen? It's Kathleen," she said softly.

My stomach remained surprisingly calm. My voice clear. My heartbeat steady. I listened. For the first time, I was willing to hear what Kathleen had to say.

She thanked me for the letter. She acknowledged my courage in writing it. She expressed her regret and sadness over everything that occurred between her and my ex-husband. I appreciated the call—and her courage in making it. But as I replaced the receiver, I noticed that none of it mattered anymore. The words I had desperately wanted to hear for so long were suddenly unimportant.

I had finally discovered what I was really looking for—the lesson that had been buried deep in the drama of my divorce. God is my source and my strength. That's what all of it—her affair with my husband, the divorce, their marriage, even my children's pain—had been about. My relationship with God.

It wasn't about Kathleen after all. It was about *me*. Her behavior had simply illuminated this deep void in my life. Everything else was secondary. At that moment I had a clear experience of what formerly had been a stack of psychological and religious information. But now everything was different. I knew with absolute certainty that no one can hurt me—not really—not if I know who I am in Christ. Every experience, no matter how painful or confusing it seems, serves my spiritual growth. Every moment, every event has its purpose.

God is my source and my strength. And He will supply all my needs. Finally I understood the meaning of words I had read many times before, *Fear not, and be not dismayed . . . for the battle is not yours but God's* (II Chronicles 20:15).

—Karen O'Connor

Showing Compassion

A year ago, I was assisting in a C.L.A.S.S. (Christian Leaders, Authors, and Speakers Seminar) as a group leader. During these three-day seminars, we divide into small groups, assigning one leader to every ten conferees.

I was the one responsible for putting people into groups. Since I knew nothing about the people at the seminar, I just prayed, "Lord, please help me employ my organizational system and then use that system to get each person into the right group."

I ended up with seven women and three men in my group. In my experiences as a group leader, I have found that women are generally more open about themselves than men. I was desirous for the entire group, including the men, to share something of their heart and life rather than just their personal accomplishments and credentials.

I prayed, "Lord, open the men up. Help them to share themselves rather than just be content to let the women share personal experiences. Don't let it scare them if the women share. Let it move them emotionally and spiritually."

I got into my group that afternoon and proceeded in my normal fashion. In the first session we have each person introduce himself or herself to the group. I usually ask, "Who would like to be first?" because I don't like to put people on the spot.

While the group prepared for their three-minute introductions, I felt the Lord say to me, *Start with the lady on your right.*

I don't do that, Lord, I hastily replied. *You know I don't like to put people on the spot. What if she says, "NO, I don't want to do it yet"?*

I kept hearing the Lord say, *Start with the lady on your right.*

So I very timidly asked, "Would you like to be first?"

She eagerly said, "Yes, I'd like to."

When she started to speak, she began to cry. She looked at

me and said, "I knew I was going to be in your group, and I told the Lord I didn't want to be here."

I thought, *I wonder what's going on? Maybe she's lost a child, but why wouldn't she want to be in my group?*

She continued, "My son was in a car accident last December. His fiancee was killed. My son was a drunk driver."

As the mother of a son who was killed by a drunk driver, immediately my heart and my head were battling harsh feelings: *If I'd known about that, I wouldn't have put you in my group. I would've given you to someone else.*

She started talking about how difficult her situation was. Her son was facing a seven-month jail term.

I was thinking, *Only seven months? Why didn't he get seven years?*

Then the Lord spoke to me, *Marilyn, I want you to comfort this lady.*

I looked at her as she was sobbing and talking about all the difficult things she was facing. Normally I'd be hugging and comforting someone going through pain like that. But this time I thought, *No, I can't do that. I think her son ought to go to jail. I don't really feel too sorry for her.*

The Lord began to do a work in me right there. He said, *Marilyn, you said you've forgiven the drunk driver. You've said you trusted Me in this situation. Trust Me with this lady and show compassion to her.*

I finally stood up and walked over to her in faith. I had no idea what I was going to say. I didn't know if I could get anything out. I looked at her and said, "As a mother of a son who was killed by a drunk driver, I want you to know that I love you." Then I hugged her. The woman sobbed and sobbed and fell into my arms. As I looked around at the group, I realized there wouldn't be a problem with the men opening up. They weren't just shedding tears, they were sobbing. I have never had a group open up as that group did.

As we got around to the last lady in the group, she stood up and said, "I knew God was going to put me in your group, and I wanted to be here. I'm from Carrollton, Kentucky. I have just been working with the families of the twenty-seven people who were killed in the bus fire caused by a drunk driver. I have been doing everything I can to see to it that the drunk driver stayed in jail for the rest of his life. Today God has shown me that there are two sides to every story.

She walked over to the lady whose son was a drunk driver and they hugged each other tightly. When we were finished, I walked out of that room and Florence Littauer looked at me and said, "Are you all right?"

I replied, "No."

She said, "Do you want to talk about it?"

"No!"

I ran to my room and cried, "Lord, that wasn't fair. You put me in such a difficult position. It wasn't easy to show compassion to that mother."

God gently replied, *Marilyn, you had a rough edge which needed to be smoothed off. You need to have compassion for a lady like this. She is one of My children too, and she's hurting right now.*

The next day, the lady came to the group and said, "I need to speak first and I need to talk about my son again. I know this is hard on you, but will you please let me talk?"

I nodded and she said, "I want you to know my husband and I are born-again Christians. We raised our children in a Christian home. We don't understand what happened. Ever since my son's accident, I have thought somehow it must be my fault."

Her words struck a familiar cord. She was just like the rest of us. She was a victim, too.

She continued, "I have been thinking, I need somebody to forgive me, somebody to love me. Yesterday you did and you released me."

—Marilyn Willett Heavilin

5

Overcoming Obstacles

*Therefore, my dear brothers, stand firm. Let nothing move
you. Always give yourselves fully to the work of the Lord,
because you know that your labor in the Lord is not in vain.*

I Corinthians 15:58

Back In The Air Again

Another new one. Again. I huffed one of my brave-martyr sighs at the cat, but Punkin paid no heed—he'd heard it all before. I enjoyed living by myself, but I dreaded the constant hassle of training new home health aides.

Bam. Bam. Bam. Show time, Vickie! I wheeled to the door and pulled it open. When the young woman stepped inside, I did a double take.

She grinned. "Not what you were expecting, am I?"

"Well, ah . . . no," I stammered while my face turned various shades of red. With a name like Mae Lynne, I had pictured a soft-spoken, dainty slip of a girl, her black hair tied back with a pink ribbon. The attractive woman with beautiful red curly hair who had insistently pounded on my door did not fit the stereotype.

I talked Mae Lynne through my transfer from the wheelchair to the bed and our conversation turned to skydiving. I explained the relatively new concept of tandem skydiving—where an experienced skydiving instructor wears a harness with an over-sized dual parachute pack.

"The back of the student's harness attaches to hardware on the front of the instructor's harness," I told her enthusiastically. "Both student and instructor face the same direction and leave the plane as one. The instructor can pull the ripcord to deploy the chute, steer the canopy, and land without help from the student. That makes skydiving a possibility for me."

"Before my husband and I got married," my new aide confided, "We had the money all saved up to make a jump. Then it went for something else. Now we have three kids and we never did get around to making that jump."

"How about when I make a jump, you make one too," I said.

"Sure!" she said.

"By the way," I added, "Two weeks from Saturday I'm making

a tandem skydive." Seeing her incredulous expression, I grinned. "Not what you were expecting, am I?"

Two weeks later, I made the jump and the grin on my face became a permanent fixture—even after I was safely tucked in bed that night. I grasped a mouthstick firmly between my teeth, turned toward the speaker phone, and tapped a few buttons. A pre-programmed number efficiently dialed itself.

"Hello," a familiar voice chimed. "You jumped out of an airplane, wow!"

This woman has me pegged pretty well, and she handles my antics "awful good" for a mom. A month ago I told Mom about tandem skydiving and asked her if she wanted to know ahead of time should I ever make a jump. She briefly considered and said, "No." Being the conscientious daughter that I am, I honored her request.

"Tell me all about it!" Mom's voice broke into my thoughts.

Hmmm . . . where to begin. My mind drifted back to the various events leading up to this day. One of my true loves of the past was skydiving. At seventeen I made a solo jump and got hooked. Twelve years and 300 jumps later, paralysis had made me stop skydiving and take up sitting.

The planning for this jump began last spring when an old skydiving buddy, Stan, materialized on my doorstep during a short layover. While we reminisced, the topic of tandem skydiving came up. Soon, Stan located an airport willing to accommodate me. And "The Day" finally arrived.

Mae Lynne drove me out to the airport. This marked my first time at a drop zone since before the accident. Jumpers eyed my cumbersome electric wheelchair and their somber thoughts echoed through the deafening silence: "There but for the grace of God . . ." But their uneasiness didn't last long. Soon fellow skydivers swapped jump stories with me and I felt right at home.

My instructor, Rick, explained the procedure for making the jump, then two jumpers helped wrestle my body into a jumpsuit and harness. Another carried me to the plane and set me inside.

Riding up to altitude in the Cessna 206 felt like the most normal thing I'd done since my accident.

At 10,500 feet above the ground, Rick opened the door, moved us closer, and let our legs dangle out. The sight almost took my breath away: sunshine, clear skies, lots of altitude. What a delicious yet almost forgotten feeling. After all, quadriplegics aren't supposed to go leaping out of airplanes, are they?

I heard the command, "Cut!" The pilot reduced the speed, Rick leaned forward, and we were out. Falling free. Free falling! Memories flooded over me as the wind rushed past. Plummeting toward earth, we built up speed. I had forgotten how difficult breathing can become when hurtling through space at 120 miles per hour.

At 4500 feet, when the tiny specks on the ground began to resemble human beings, Rick pulled the ripcord. Pow! The parachute slammed open and I reeled from the abrupt jolt. I hadn't remembered opening shock as such a bone-wrenching experience. My teeth felt loose!

Quietly we floated gently down, reminding me of the "hush" I'd experienced on my first jump over a decade ago.

The parachute danced in the sparkling blue sky as all too soon we made one last turn to set up an approach pattern. A light breeze made for a perfect stand-up landing. Rick touched down and two jumpers reached out to steady us. I had done it! I had actually done it!

After imparting every last detail to my mother, I finally hung up. On the whole, I think she's greatly relieved that quadriplegia has slowed me down so much. At least she doesn't worry anymore about me breaking my neck. Come to think of it, neither do I!

—Vickie Baker

Depending On God

I once met a woman in counseling who didn't think she could depend on God in the same way she used to depend on her doting father. Sherie was single, 36 years old, and with tears she challenged God and me. "You say God loves me and can meet all of my needs and fill my cup," she said. "But who's going to take care of me? Who's going to talk to me? Who's He providing for me?" Then she added, "I have a car stereo that won't fit my car. It was a gift so I can't return it, and I don't even know the first thing to do about it. Now tell me how God can meet a need like that?"

I did not know how God would meet her needs, but I knew He could, even with her stereo. "Are you willing to ask God to become the source of your life and to depend on Him for every need?" I asked her. At first she couldn't do it because she still felt God had cheated her. We got on our knees and with tears she prayed, "God, I want to depend on you but I can't." After two more tries, she finally blurted out, "Okay, God, I will completely trust my life in Your hands and let You, in Your timing, fill my life and take care of my everyday needs."

That encounter left her emotionally exhausted and I honestly did not expect much to happen for while. But the next morning she could hardly wait to call me. She had called a retailer to see if she could exchange her stereo. The store manager said he didn't carry that model but suggested that she call the factory office. She did. It was after working hours so a regional manager answered the phone. After some discussion, he recognized her name. Her father had been one of his closest friends in high school. "If you're his daughter," he said, "I'll take complete care of whatever you need."

Stunned, Sherie recognized this as a demonstration of God's faithfulness. In subsequent years she has filled several notebooks detailing how God has met her specific needs.

—**Gary Smalley**

No One Is Useless

It was New Year's Day—the day my friend Almeda should have been celebrating her thirty-sixth wedding anniversary. Instead, she was opening Christmas gifts.

"Mother, why not use both hands?" her daughter Clarice suggested.

The words stuck in Almeda's throat. "I can't."

Sometime during the two weeks that she had been hospitalized for cerebral aneurysm, she had suffered a massive stroke. At age 58, her left side was completely paralyzed.

Devastated just months before by an unwanted divorce, and desperately lonely, Almeda learned to walk with a folding cane after months of painful therapy. When the doctor said she would never again use her withered left hand, she begged God to please let her die. When the time came for her to be dismissed from the hospital, her therapist suggested she go first to a nursing home for a period of adjustment. She refused.

"Clarice can look after me," she stubbornly told her family.

Her adult children hired a woman to come in each day to help. Almeda dismissed her.

Clarice, however, was in classes all day at the university. Mired in self-pity, it did not occur to Almeda that what she considered "being independent" was making life difficult for her young daughter. Alone each day, with little to do but stare at her useless hand, she grew increasingly bitter.

Hardly a day passed without a cheerful suggestion from Clarice intended to ease her mother's pain.

"Momma, you know you've always loved to read. Please let me get you some books from the library," she begged one morning.

"I don't feel like reading."

"Well, I wish you'd do something! You used to be always doing for others. Now the only one you ever think about is yourself!"

Clarice was instantly contrite. "Mom, I'm sorry. I know I can't really know what it's like to be—"

Ignoring her stricken expression, Almeda finished for her. "A cripple—a useless divorcee—a has-been."

The door had barely closed behind Clarice before Almeda sensed God's disapproval. She had been a Christian for years. God had comforted her through the pain of divorce. In the hospital and at home, she had told others of His loving care and praised Him for every inch of progress. Filled with shame over her cranky behavior, for the first time in months, her thoughts turned outward.

Clarice was barely 19. How hard it must be for her to be so tied down. Looking ruefully at the wasted claw that had once buttoned her tiny dresses, my contrite friend willed the hand, somehow, to be restored to usefulness.

The hand, of course, would never do for Clarice again. Neither would Almeda pick up children for Sunday school or teach her class of three-year-olds. Her will, however, was a different matter. Certainly she could apologize and try to be more cooperative and less of a grump. Intending that very moment to begin thinking more positive thoughts, she leaned back in her favorite brocade chair and closed her eyes.

Immediately, she "saw" a jar of farm-canned beef her sister-in-law had recently given them. Although breakfast had happened but a short time before, her mouth watered as she thought of those succulent chunks of tender meat bubbling in rich broth.

Clarice loved stew. But a good stew must have time to simmer. While as usual, Clarice would be home at noon, she would have scant time to do more than prepare a hasty lunch for the two of them.

Rising, grasping the doorjamb for support, Almeda limped slowly to the kitchen and took down the cutting board. Jutting from its center was a big steel nail, a grim reminder of her disability. With her good hand, she pulled the bag of potatoes from beneath the sink, rinsed a large one, pushed it down onto the nail and painstakingly began to peel.

"Oh, Mom, you're going to get well!" Clarice whooped when she came in at noon and smelled the stew cooking. Encouraged, and a little bit proud of herself, Almeda began trying her hand with other foods. As her cooking skills returned, she thought of the neighbors and friends who had been so kind during her long illness. Her therapist had taught her how to break eggs. With the aid of her nail and a non-skid pad to keep the bowl from traveling, she mixed a batch of cookies. Battling the hot pans and heavy oven door took most of the afternoon. But when she handed that plate piled high with soft coconut cookies to her next-door neighbor, her heart swelled with the half-forgotten joy of giving.

She baked more cookies and gave most of them away. From grapes that grew in her backyard, she made jelly in safe-to-handle, two-cup batches. It, too, was for sharing. Gradually, she learned to give of herself by phoning shut-ins. A listening ear became her special ministry to victims of divorce and stroke.

For Almeda, some things may never change. She remains divorced when she would rather be married. Her hand is still useless and always will be. But Almeda is not.

No one is, not in God's sight.

"I'm so glad," says Almeda, "That God gave me a yearning for stew."

—C. Ellen Watts

They Found Him

When the children were three-year-old neighbors they fought over toys. But wise parents instructed them about the need to share by teaching them to take turns. Thus they discovered the joy of mutual respect!

When they were seven, and the training wheels came off their two-wheelers, after each spill they picked each other up with a word of encouragement. They discovered the joy of compassion!

When they were eight they competed in Little League, learning that some are strong hitters, others fast runners, and only a few are skilled pitchers. They discovered the joy of tolerance!

When they were ten and taking their first swimming lesson they held their breath in the scary, silent underwater, and grasped their hands together tightly. They discovered the joy of having someone to count on!

When they were twelve they built their first skateboards, pooling money and talents for parts and labor. They discovered the joy of patience and team work!

When they were fourteen they started high school, sharing lockers and lunches; books and basketballs. They discovered the joy of adolescent friendship!

When they were sixteen and sitting behind the wheel of the family car for the first time, they tasted freedom. They learned the joy of responsibility!

When they were eighteen they entered college, enrolling at different schools miles apart. They discovered the joy of supportive pen pals!

When they were twenty-four, in the presence of excited families and friends, they witnessed each other's church weddings. They discovered the joy of God's blessings on marriage!

When they were twenty-six they compared baby pictures, proudly presenting their first-borns to each other. They discovered the joy of fatherhood!

But when they were thirty and trying to buy adjoining homes outside the community where they were raised, one was rejected—although both qualified for the required bank loan. They discovered the pangs of prejudice!

In their frustration they turned to God in prayer and were blessed with wisdom and strength with which to cope and correct. They discovered the joy of a spiritual renewal marked by a faith more mature than anything they experienced in their childhood! It was a faith to sustain the challenges of adulthood and parenting, enabling them to pass on the values their parents instilled in them.

—Jean Rodgers

Unclaimed Gifts

I once heard a story about a man who died and was given a guided tour of heaven by St. Peter. When they came to an immense warehouse filled with all shapes and sizes of wrapped packages, the man asked Peter what they were. Peter replied sadly, "This is where God keeps all the gifts He intended for His children. These were never claimed." Unfortunately, many today never claim God's promised packages. We leave His gifts in the warehouse of heaven, either because we never ask or because we get out of line too soon.

—**Gary Smalley**

Codependency

Lord, I can no longer live
   In an empty past.
   Barely existing in surroundings
   Long forgotten by You.
   I need to go back . . .
   Just one more time.
   Not to wallow in the pain
   But to bury the dead;
   The false guilt of failure
   I carry still today.
   Lord, give me the courage
   to face them without fear
   confront them without anger
   and leave them without shame.
   Allow me the wisdom it will take
   To return without self-pity
   trust without compromise
   And continue without blame.
   Father, please, give me insight
   so that at last, I can claim
   the future I deserve.
   Standing firm in my convictions;
   Answering only for today.

—**Marcia Krugh Leaser**

Grabbing Hold Of Fulfillment

Never underestimate the power of a woman who has yielded her life to God. She not only has strength but a special, radiating beauty. Norma had that glow during our courtship and when we were first married. After several years of marriage, however, her power and beauty started to fade, and she blamed me for her lack of fulfillment.

Norma was frustrated with me for good reason. I traveled nearly fifty percent of the time and was so consumed with work that I had little energy left for her and the kids. When Michael, our third child, was born, he was sick much of the time and so Norma could not maintain the house and care for the children without my help. She tried conventional methods to get me to change. She talked to me, she pleaded, she cried. Nothing worked. I didn't change, and neither did she. But then Norma tried something *unconventional*. Her action motivated me to ask for a different position in the company so I could spend more time at home.

What was this powerful action she took?

Norma had read about God's love for her. He had demonstrated His love by sending Jesus Christ, His only Son, to give her abundant life. By demanding that I change, she was in essence saying that she could not experience a full life unless God somehow used me to meet her needs. But God was ready and willing to meet her needs, apart from me, if she would only let Him.

With no coaching from me, Norma changed her thinking, admitted she hadn't been seeking God alone, and began her own journey to find God's fulfilling love. Rather than complain to me, she prayed, "Lord, thank You that all I need is You. You know I want a good relationship with Gary and that I want him to spend more time at home. You also know that I'm not very strong physically. I'm so tired that I don't feel I can last much longer under this strain. I'm coming to You with these requests because I know that if I need Gary at home, *You* can either make it happen or take away my desire. I'm going to stop fighting Gary and instead ask You either to change him or to meet my needs in some other way."

To find God's fulfillment, Norma took steps similar to those I later discovered. She stopped expecting life from me and started looking to God. She realized I not only would not, but could not, fill her life, so she went to the source of life and asked Him to fill her.

The results were startling. I noticed the change almost immediately. When I came home from work, I sensed a calm spirit in our house. Norma's face was peaceful, no longer tense. Instead of the usual harsh words, her conversation was quiet and she was more interested in asking me how my day had gone than in relating her activities with the children.

After a few days, I couldn't keep from asking what had happened. "Gary, I got tired of fighting you," she explained calmly. "I realized that I wasn't trusting God concerning our marriage and family, and so I decided to stop complaining and start praying. I've told God that I would like you to spend more time at home, and if I really need that, I know He will make the necessary changes." She also grabbed my attention by stating, in a calm and undemanding way, "I think I'm headed for a physical collapse. Michael has been sick so much, and with the other responsibilities, I don't think I can last much longer."

Imagine what that did to me. I was instantly convicted that my priorities were wrong. And that wasn't all. Because Norma had changed, I *wanted* to spend more time at home. That same week I asked to change my job so I could spend more time meeting my family's needs.

—Gary Smalley

On The Anvil

With a strong forearm, the apron-clad blacksmith puts his tongs into the fire, grasps the heated metal, and places it on his anvil. His keen eye examines the glowing piece. He sees what the tool is now and envisions what he wants it to be—sharper, flatter, wider, longer. With a clear picture in his mind, he begins to pound. His left hand still clutching the hot mass with the tongs, the right hand slams the two-pound sledge upon the moldable metal.

On the solid anvil, the smoldering iron is remolded.

The smith knows the type of instrument he wants. He knows the size. He knows the shape. He knows the strength.

Whang! Whang! The hammer slams. The shop rings with noise, the air fills with smoke, and the softened metal responds.

But the response doesn't come easily. It doesn't come without discomfort. To melt down the old and recast it as new is a disrupting process. Yet the metal remains on the anvil, allowing the toolmaker to remove the scars, repair the cracks, refill the voids, and purge the impurities.

And with time, a change occurs: What was dull becomes sharpened, what was crooked becomes straight, what was weak becomes strong, and what was useless becomes valuable.

Then the blacksmith stops. He ceases his pounding and sets down his hammer. With a strong left arm, he lifts the tongs until the freshly molded metal is at eye level. In the still silence, he examines the smoking tool. The incandescent implement is rotated and examined for any mars or cracks.

There are none.

Now the smith enters the final stage of his task. He plunges the smoldering instrument into a nearby bucket of water. With a hiss and a rush of steam, the metal immediately begins to harden. The heat surrenders to the onslaught of cool water, and the pliable, soft mineral becomes an unbending, useful tool.

For a little while you may have had to suffer grief in all kinds of trials. These have come so that your faith—of greater worth than golf, which perishes even though refined by fire—may be proved genuine and may result in praise, glory and honor when Jesus Christ is revealed (I Peter 1:6-7).

—Max Lucado

The Gift Of Forgiveness

One night while I was sleeping, an angel came to me
She handed me a package, and in it was a key.

The key was made of solid gold, and Freedom was its name
Forgiveness was its purpose, for they are both the same.

"This will free you from all bondage, forgiveness makes it so
The Lord sent it as a gift, to heal you from each blow.

He knew you would encounter many hurts in life,
your road would be a rough one, filled with pain and strife.

This key is multipurpose, it does so many things.
It heals and frees your spirit, and pays homage to your King."

The Key

I can't begin to tell you how oft I need this key
Nor can I convey, how much it means to me.

Sometimes when I am angry, I WILL NOT, to pick it up
Until my heart's so heavy, that I fetch it from its cup.

It's there for me to use each day, a gift from God you know
It clears my heart of bitterness, when I let the anger go.

I burn myself quite often, by holding on too tight
And toss and turn with outrage, all through the night.

Not until I use this key, can I find peace of mind
Forgiveness, is God's answer for abuse of every kind.

—Cheryl Williams

Hitting The Wall

It was April 17, 1989, near the end of the twenty-six and one-half mile Boston Marathon; my body had "hit the wall." But somehow, the combination of cheers from the million and a half plus crowd and the atmosphere of energy that knifed the air made my spirit fly! I had fulfilled the unreachable, impossible dream.

For a brief flash I thought of the "carbo party" held the previous evening at the Black Falcon Terminal, overlooking shimmering lights on the Bay where I chatted with a distinguished gentleman sitting in front of me.

"Say, Rich, tell me about your accident."

I stared at him! How could he know?

"I couldn't help but notice the little scars on your forehead. You have been in a halo. I'm a surgeon."

Of course, a doctor would notice. Memories surfaced as I told him my story.

On April 4, 1984, I was returning from a drinking party near Chico State University, in Chico, California. I was nineteen years old and life was a party! I had rebelled against the God of my parents, even though Dad had tried to reason with me many times.

To avoid hitting a dog, I slammed on the brakes of my soft-top CJ5. The jeep rolled two times, then landed on me and another passenger. The back of my neck hit the curb, and a wrench pierced my side, leaving a deep hole. My skull took a beating from the impact, leaving a crack from my ear to the top of my head. My pelvis was broken in four places. I had turned blue when a bystander revived me with artificial resuscitation.

The shrill ringing of the phone reached Mother and Dad at one-thirty in the morning. "There's been an accident. Your son is in the hospital, in a coma and not expected to live." Fighting panic, they raced to the hospital and inadvertently walked into the emergency room to see their son comatose and bloody.

In the waiting room, the attending neurosurgeon explained,

"The X-rays show no spinal chord in the injured area, which indicates that it is severed there. His neck is broken in four places and the vertebrae are separated. I'm sorry, but he could slip away at any moment. I doubt if we can save him. But if he does survive, he will never function as a normal person."

Temporarily shaken, my parents were strengthened by arriving friends, family, and from hearing that prayer chains for me had begun.

Toward morning the neurosurgeon said, "These X-rays are beginning to look better. Whatever it is that you're doing, keep it up."

Miraculously, I survived the night and moved to the trauma unit for treatment. But my life hung on a thread during the days that followed. I had been placed on a breathing machine and developed pneumonia, a major crisis. At one point a high fever developed and the doctors thought it was the end. Time and time again God intervened as many people throughout California and Washington prayed.

The following Sunday morning Dad attended church where the congregation had been praying. An elderly woman greeted him and quoted Psalm 117, *He shall live and not die*. Greatly comforted, Dad would need that scripture later because a blood clot had formed on my brain and was expanding. Without an operation I would surely die. But in my condition I was not expected to survive an operation. Again I surprised the doctors when I *did* live.

The doctors prepared my parents for my recovery saying, "He will be nothing more than a vegetable, unable to walk or talk." Mother and Dad continued to pray.

Twenty-eight days after the injury I came out of the coma. "He's talking—and spelling!" The news circled throughout the hospital. Medical science could not explain such a recovery.

I entered the Therapeutic Treatment Center at Chico Community Hospital, but the sincere sympathy of the nurses incensed me: "Rich, you must learn to accept your limitations."

Live like this? Not me! Their words challenged me and I

worked diligently during therapy, determined with the help of Almighty God to walk. And in four weeks I could walk alone.

Two months after the accident, the doctors wanted to remove the "halo" (a device screwed into the head, with a circle that goes around the head to prevent movement of the vertebrae) but they were concerned because one of the vertebrae was out of alignment. So they scheduled an operation on my neck.

The night before the surgery I attended a prayer meeting and was anointed with oil and baptized in the Holy Spirit. I actually felt a surge of power through my neck during prayer and knew God had touched me. The next morning when the doctors X-rayed, they discovered the vertebrae were in position. I was elated but realized I did not deserve God's mercy. I was motivated to learn about Him for myself.

One year after the accident, the doctors allowed me to run again. It was like setting fire to a furnace. In four months I competed in a triathlon and, since then, have competed in many different kinds of races.

Beyond exhaustion as I raced the last few yards down Boston's Boylston Street. I wanted to etch this moment into my mind forever. After nearly collapsing across the finish line, I was amazed to discover that amid the competition of Olympic and professional runners, I had finished in the top twenty percent. As I received that medal around my neck, I sent a prayer of thanks heavenward. Tears ran down my cheeks. *Is there anything You can't do, my Father in heaven?*

—Rich Sprenkel, Jr.

Waiting In The Fog

Father,
  I don't like this!
  Mist has fogged all certainty.
  I can't *see*!
  There are no colors,
  Not even black and white,
  just . . . gray.
  No clear-cut outlines,
  No vision of purpose or plans,
  just cold, wet mist.

I'm terrified, lost, feeling abandoned.
But within my heart I know that,
though I can't see You,
your eye is on me.
Your hand holds mine . . .
even though its touch
is lost to me right now.

And from somewhere comes the
knowledge that in my
quest for humility—
Your desire for my humility—
The mist is part of the path.

Not knowing,
not understanding,
not seeing,
are tools—important ones—
for teaching me . . . well,
as yet I know not what.

The mist diffuses Your Light—
walls it back to me,

confuses the source of that Light.
I'm unable even to look down
to see the Rock beneath my feet
I can only stand still
and wait
and listen
and *hope.*

—Carole Mayhall

Rebellion And Cancer

My fifteen-and-a-half-year-old daughter, Darcy, was going through a rebellious time. She had always been strong-willed and her teenage years were the epitome of her wanting-to-be-in-control viewpoint of life. She had begun talking on the phone with a seventeen-year-old friend from school about his girlfriend quite regularly. At times he would take her out to talk about his problems. Before we knew it, Darcy had become the new girlfriend, even though she wasn't supposed to date until she turned sixteen.

Whenever my husband, Larry, and I reminded her of our rule, she turned surly and argumentative. Every evening that she left, she shouted at us, "You want to know why I'm leaving all the time? I hate being here. I can't wait until I turn 18, I'm outta here!"

I was stunned by her behavior. Why is she so angry at us? What is going on in the relationship between this boy and Darcy? Is she staying true to the purity we taught her? Time and again we tried to reach out to her. I felt worried and helpless; nothing seemed to make any difference. Each time we tried to talk to her, she closed off emotionally and wouldn't respond.

Unfortunately, that wasn't the only worry we were facing at that time. A mole on Larry's chest had been growing and changing color. Our doctor, Dr. Hanson, examined it and said it could be melanoma—the deadliest kind of skin cancer. That struck a fearful chord within us since a good friend of ours had died of melanoma three years earlier. Dr. Hanson removed the mole and sent it to the lab for a biopsy. We waited, wanting to believe the results would be negative but knowing in our hearts it was cancer. The test results confirmed it was melanoma. Within a few days, more tissue would have to be removed to determine if the cancer had gone inside his body.

"Is Larry's life in danger? Will I become a widow at such an early age?" I wondered. I prayed over and over again, "Lord God, I don't want to lose my best friend." We were shaken, worry tried to turn my wondering into fear, yet God gave us a peace that we could trust His plan for Larry's life.

After the additional tissue was removed and sent for testing, we again waited for the test results. As we did, Darcy's rebellious attitude continued to create additional tension in our family. One evening, Larry and I decided we had to try again to reach out to her. Calling her into our bedroom, we asked her to sit in the chair while we sat against the headboard on our bed. As soon as Darcy sat down, she crossed her arms and glared at us, seemingly defying us to break through her cold and distant perspective.

"Darcy, honey, we love you," Larry began. "We want to know what's going on so that we can work through our differences."

Darcy sat immobilized, her face just as impassive as ever. I spoke up, "Darcy, we really do want to talk this out. We love and care about you. Please let us know how you're feeling and what the problem is." Darcy still sat silent, her lips pursed in defiance.

Larry and I looked at each other feeling hopeless and helpless. "Oh, God," I prayed silently. "Please help us. What will get through to her?"

Larry and I continued to talk to Darcy. Then without any explanation, her face softened, her arms came down and she began talking to us. We were thrilled! For forty-five minutes we talked and talked. We found out she wanted to keep a pure relationship with that boy and that her values were similar to ours. As we all talked, Larry and I shot glances at each other with a look that questioned, "Why is she finally talking with us?" We had no idea.

When we were finished, Darcy stood up and walked over to the bedroom door. She put her hand on the knob, opened it slightly and then hesitated. She looked back at us with a confused look and said, "I don't know why I'm talking to you like this." Then as if the reason had occurred to her, she continued, "But it's because Daddy has cancer."

God had used for good what we thought could never be used for good: cancer. As a strong-willed teenager, the Lord knew that only something as severe as possibly losing her Daddy to cancer would make her see life with a different perspective. Darcy never returned to that state of rebellion and today we all have a fantastic relationship. She is a college graduate, a delightful young woman who loves God, and the co-author with me in a book, *Staying Friends With Your Kids* (Harold Shaw Publishers). We rejoice that Larry has been free of melanoma for over six years. God knows how to work in people's lives and we've seen that to be true in our family.

As He has so faithfully shown us many times before, He *causes all things to work together for good to those who love God and are called according to His purpose* (Romans 8:28).

Since then, I've claimed that promise over and over again as a solution to worry. Even if what I worry about comes true, God promises to use it for good. Therefore I don't have to worry because it's really all in God's plan and purposes.

—Kathy Collard Miller

6

Reaching Out During Hurt

Rejoice with those who rejoice; mourn with those who mourn.

Romans 12:15

The Voice Of My Heart

My heart pounded like a locomotive at top speed as I exited off the freeway into the Watts section of Los Angeles. I was searching for the garden area next to Martin Luther King Jr. Hospital on this Saturday, January 29, 1994, when a voice inside my head screamed, "Are you crazy? What are you doing in this neighborhood alone, you short, defenseless white woman?" I turned up the radio trying to drown out the fear and refocused my attention on the address.

"Oh, no, I passed it," I muttered out loud. Searching for a place to turn around, I noticed a group of four African-American men standing on a corner talking. The voice in my head screamed louder than the music, "Remember, Reginald Denny was almost killed less than a year ago—not too far from here!"

I concentrated on my driving and after taking a side street back, found the garden area of the hospital. I turned off the radio, and heard drum beats when the familiar voice of my husband called to me. My heartbeat slowed like a train arriving in town. I had not seen him for a week and he looked scraggly and unshaven, yet his smile glowed with love.

As we walked toward a group of men, he told me that during the first few days at this multi-cultural men's conference to stop violence, he had been pretty scared. Pointing to a young, tall African-American man he explained, "He was one of the angriest and most outspoken men at the conference. He is really angry at white society." I kept my eye on this young man as we gathered in a huge circle in the garden.

This group of mostly African-American men, with some Hispanics, and a few Asians and Caucasians, had invited their families to the closing celebration of their week-long conference. I stood with thirty women and children interspersed within the circle of one hundred men as they sang songs from South America, West Africa and Native America. I felt separate, a bystander, not really included.

I noticed three of the leaders approach the young man I was

watching. I sensed something wrong. They pulled him aside and talked quietly with him. He fell to his knees, sobbing. The leaders held him, comforting him while the rest of the group continued to sing joyously about breaking down barriers and prejudices.

Michael Mead, one of the leaders, joined the circle and motioned to the drummers to stop as the other leaders and the young man entered the circle.

"A tragic thing has happened," Michael called out. "This celebration needs to be changed to include a memorial for our brother here. We just found out that his cousin was shot to death today in a drive-by shooting."

The drums began to beat slowly, and the men began to sing. As I watched the hurting young man, a still, small voice in my heart whispered, "Go hug him." I silently screamed back, "No way! Me, a short, white woman, walk through the middle of this circle and go up to hug this man? Women aren't even a part of this community."

"Go hug him," the voice whispered again. I stood, feeling as if my feet were cemented into the grass. When the singing stopped, my heart cried out, "Oh no, I missed my chance."

The drums began to beat slowly and the men started singing again. I took a deep breath, let go of my husband's arm, and stepped through the center of the circle. Everyone else blurred out of focus as I moved toward this hurting man. As I approached him, I looked up into his big brown eyes and lifted my arms up to him. He gazed into my eyes, slowly bent down and reached out to me. We embraced each other for minutes; it seemed like eternity. He sang an old, spiritual song, his voice making a beautiful, loving sound in my ear. When we released our embrace, we gazed into each others' eyes like a mother and son expressing a love that no other could destroy.

Then, I walked to my place within the circle. Turning back around, I saw a man embracing him, and a line of men waiting to comfort the grieving young man.

—Dr. Lorrie Boyd

Representing Jesus

As I walked across the parking lot into the hospital that hot, August afternoon, I asked God to use me to bring His love to my patients. As a nurse, I had many opportunities to pray for patients and their families, and to be a vessel for God's use. My heart was hurting this particular day for one of my patients: a young man, with a precious wife and a dear little tow-headed, two-year-old son. Donald had been diagnosed with leukemia about a year ago, and the nursing staff had witnessed his body's gradual decline. Now in his last days, his beautiful young wife remained by his bedside. Frequently she would slip out of his room, lean against the wall and weep. If their little two-year-old was there, he would wrap his chubby arms around her legs and ask, "Mommy, why are you sad?"

When Donald was first admitted to the hospital, he had been pleasant and friendly, but with each successive admission for chemotherapy, he became more angry and withdrawn. Each visit kept him longer and longer, and whenever he was my patient, I prayed, "God, give me the right words to say, and help him to be open to hearing about You." He always remained polite, but curt, and left very little opportunity for me to share with him.

That morning at church, the guest speaker had shared from Matthew 25:42-44 and talked about when we minister to others, we also minister to Jesus. I could understand the idea of blessing others with Jesus, but wasn't too clear about ministering to Him. So I had prayed that morning for God to show me how to minister and bless Him. But that was the farthest thing from my mind as I arrived at work.

That evening at 8:00 p.m. I started going from room-to-room getting my assigned patients ready for the night. I came to Donald's room, and as I entered his doorway, I pleaded with God to open Donald's heart and to help me minister to him. I felt that this could be my last time to care for him. Now only skin and bones, every vertebra and joint showed through his transparent skin. He always sat up because it was impossible for him to breath if he laid down. He leaned forward over a padded T-shaped frame that a friend had made for him. The room was dim and quiet, except for his labored breathing. I gave him his medications, hung a new IV bottle and straightened his bed.

"Donald," I quietly said, "What can I do to make you more comfortable?"

He replied in a soft, raspy whisper, more like a man of advanced years than a man in his late 20's, "Please rub my back, it hurts so much."

As I carefully rubbed lotion on his back, I began to pray for him, and asked God again for the right words. But no words came. I closed my eyes and focused on Jesus as I continued gently massaging his fragile back. Donald seemed to be relaxing a little, his breathing quieter and slower. A feeling of peacefulness invaded the room. I opened my eyes, and instead of Donald in the bed, there sat Jesus! I closed my eyes quickly. I must be mistaken! I peeked again—*Yes, it is Jesus!* I kept rubbing the back of Jesus and a feeling of perfect peace invaded the room. Then very slowly, Donald appeared back in his bed.

By now, he had fallen asleep and I quietly left the room. *Oh, thank you, Jesus. I don't know how it happened that I saw You, I just know I did!* I realized in that moment that when we are available and willing to serve others, we are truly ministering to Jesus.

—Penny Carlevato

When You Don't Know How They Feel

The other day I heard a Christian woman describe how a friend had made several "mistakes" while trying to comfort her during a time of difficulty. She complained that her friend offered advice, solutions and even dared to quote Scripture.

When I first was diagnosed as having cancer several years ago, many friends, family and even strangers reached out to me. What if, instead, they all had avoided me for fear of making a "mistake"?

The longer I live, the more grateful I am for the efforts people made to comfort me during my illness with cancer. I will never forget those who reached out to me, when from their standpoint, comforting me was the last thing they wanted to do that day. Those friends will always be special to me because they did reach out. They weren't afraid of making a "mistake." Some of them had deep, insightful things to say and responded with thoughtful actions.

After my surgery a friend came to visit me in the hospital. Later I wondered if I would have taken the initiative to visit a friend who had just been through the darkest day of her life. I am so grateful that she wasn't afraid to care.

She was a new Christian with very little Christian background. But as she sat beside my bed she happened to speak "for God" when she said, "I think that you're going to have to let some of your friends carry your pain for you." I found great comfort in her desire to help me carry my pain. And in her own way, she did.

During my battle with cancer hundreds of people communicated with me. Many of them quoted Jeremiah 29:11 to me: *For I know the plans I have for you, declares the Lord, plans to prosper you and not to harm you, plans to give you hope and a future.* I was blessed each time I read this verse. I never thought, "Surely they could come up with a more original verse!" On the contrary, the number of times this verse was given to me in my illness gave me a sense of strength that this was indeed a word from God to me.

Although there always will be a few insensitive individuals who glibly quote Scripture at random and have an answer for every instance of life, we must not overlook the fact that in times of stress and difficulty, nothing, absolutely nothing, takes the place of Scripture.

—Pat Palau

The Abandoned Apricots

By 11:30 a.m., on a sweltering Tuesday, June 23, 1992, I felt I had memorized every spot of the ICU waiting room in the Hemet, California, hospital: ceiling, floor, walls, worn furniture. And sitting on the worn furniture were all the other people waiting for news of their gravely-ill loved-ones beyond the doors of the ICU. I talked with them and prayed for them, but I was just as needy as them. *Lord, who will minister to me—and to my breaking heart?*

I, too, had a loved one behind those forbidding doors: my beloved husband, Don. I could only visit him ten minutes out of each hour, not knowing if each hour—or each minute—would be his last.

Just the Saturday before, though it seemed a million years ago now, we had driven the ninety miles from Orange County to Hemet for the day. The occasion was a big family get-together so that the West Coast relatives could meet the Midwestern children and grandchildren of my 86-year-old father-in-law's new bride.

"Bring your trumpet and keyboard along, too," Dad insisted. "I'll get out my sax and clarinet, and we'll have a little music after lunch to celebrate."

But I fussed at Don all the way there. The night before, at an Angels baseball game, he kept jumping up and twisting so ridiculously, I had demanded we leave early. Was he going to be a "pill" today, too?

Then finally we were there, meeting everyone. When lunch was delayed, our little trio went ahead and entertained with some old-time favorites. Finally, at 3 p.m., we were ready to eat. Everyone rushed to get into line, hungry, laughing, chattering away.

Everyone except Don. He had simply disappeared. When I finally found him, fifteen minutes later, he was staggering out of the bathroom in the middle of a major heart attack.

Ever since, we'd been here at the hospital. Don was trying desperately to survive with forty-five percent of his heart muscle destroyed. I was sitting around the clock, longing and praying.

Don's folks came by to see him a couple of times each day. But they were busy with that houseful of out-of-town visitors. All my friends were 90 miles away. One of my sons was up in Northern California, another seriously ill with bronchitis. The third came down as he could, but had to keep driving back to work, a couple of hours' drive each way.

Other Christians tried to comfort me. The hospital chaplain stopped by. One pastor called from Los Angeles. Dad Hanson's pastor visited. When I called in to report Don's heart attack to his insurance company, the girl answering the phone prayed with me right then. She promised to have her whole church pray, too. Not to mention concerned friends and relatives from all over the country who kept the nearby pay phone ringing off the hook.

But I was still miserable. *Why hadn't I realized that Don's "gyrations" the night before were simply attempts to shake off the pain of angina? What will I do without him?* I felt so lonely, helpless, utterly bereft.

"Dear Lord," I prayed, "I know this is impossible, but oh, I would so like to have another Christian with me, to hug me and hold my hand and pray with me!" Then, sighing, I sank back into my misery.

About an hour later, the waiting room door pushed open. A young woman entered, looking around hesitantly. Her face glistened with perspiration, her hair was tousled, her clothes covered with a large apron. An apron full of orange stains.

What in the world had brought her here in such a rush she hadn't even taken off her apron? Someone's car wreck? Or other sudden tragedy?

"E-Excuse me," she stammered, "But, uh, is anyone here waiting for a Don Hanson?"

"I-I'm Bonnie Hanson," I gasped. "But—?"

She smiled shyly and held out her hand. "Hi, I'm April. I've been sent to pray with you."

Then she explained. "See, I live in Orange County. But I've been out here all week helping my Mom can apricots. Just a while ago my husband called me from home. He said prayer chains all over the county were praying for someone named Don Hanson who was in the hospital here in Hemet.

"You're the only one I know who can help," my husband said, "Because you're already in Hemet. Why don't you go to the hospital and see if you can pray with his family?

"So I dropped the apricots, told Mom where I was going, and jumped in the car. And here I am. Let's pray." Then she took my hand, hugged me, and prayed with me.

When we'd finished, she exclaimed, "Well, better get back to my apricots." Another hug, and she was gone.

I hadn't even asked her last name!

But she left me filled with joy and peace. God *had* answered my prayer after all. *Exactly* the way I'd asked Him to! Even though I really didn't believe that He would!

He had answered through someone who never hesitated a moment when God asked her to do something that probably seemed totally off-the-wall and absurd. But she just went ahead and did it. Gladly, joyfully, as naturally as breathing. Even if it meant abandoning her apricots. And wearing a stained apron out in public!

My beloved husband did survive, and is now once more strong and full of life. How grateful we are for caring doctors, our loving Heavenly Father, our dear family, and all our Christian friends. Even those we didn't know we had.

Thank you, April!

—Bonnie Compton Hanson

A Signal At Night

The local hospital had become my new, temporary home as our 18-month-old son, John, struggled with a respiratory infection. At first John's rapid breathing and ballooning chest had caused me to tremble in fear. But after a few days of aggressive medical treatment and many prayers, John began to improve.

Even though I was thanking God with my whole heart, I was exhausted from trying to sleep on a reclining chair in John's hospital room. I missed our little three-year-old, Karen, and my husband Bob.

One particular evening Bob came to be with John and me. We chatted about John's improved condition, and how Karen was getting along at home.

All too soon Bob glanced at his watch. "Visiting hours are over; I really have to go," he said. He hugged me; then kissed me gently.

"I don't want you to leave," I said, my eyes filling with tears. "But I know you must." How I wished I could just be with my whole family again!

Bob gave me another hug. "Look down there," he said, pointing through the window to where his car was parked. "I'll be driving right past your room. Stand here at the window. When I come by, I'll blink my lights. It'll be my little signal that I love you two, and I'll be thinking of you."

Minutes later I recognized our car as it slowly moved on the street below. The lights blinked on, then off. A few more feet and another blink, and then another. As it turned onto the main street, another. The lights kept blinking until my blurred eyes could no longer see them. Then I noticed the stars of God's heavens. They were blinking too—*I love you. I love you.*

And I thought, *Isn't that the signal God wants for all of his children every night?*

—**Charlotte Adelsperger**

The Cop That God Sent

The summer of 1956, my parents had lost their full-time baby sitter. At fourteen, I took over the responsibility of my younger brothers and sister. The summer days had been exceptionally hot. As I noticed the police officer directing heavy traffic from the nearby horse races, I felt compelled to take him an ice-cold glass of juice. I found out his name was Bill and his warm smile made me feel like I'd known him for a lifetime. I learned he was married and had two children. Number three was on the way.

He loved to tease me and after a few repeat visits he told me, "You know, Karen, fights have broken out at the police department. Officers are fighting over whose turn it is to be stationed on this corner where a pretty young teenager serves cold drinks with a smile." A hot crimson flush crept over my face.

A few weeks later, a stranger came to our door, posing as a contractor. He had personal information that convinced me he had been hired by my dad. I allowed him into the house but when he got me alone he grabbed me from behind. I felt a knife blade against my throat as he said, "Don't scream or I'll kill you." A ripple of terror shot through my whole body. The rapist stole my innocence and left behind a shadow of fear that seemed to attach itself to my soul.

After he left, I escaped to a neighbors, with my sister and brothers at my side where my parents and the police were called. That afternoon, I longed to be my daddy's little girl once more, to have him hold me and tell me that I'd be all right. When he learned I'd been raped, he turned and walked away from me. The foundation of my world crumbled.

When the police questioned me, I felt more like a criminal than a victim. In the fifties there were no rape crisis centers or support groups. My parents had their own pain and were unable to meet my needs. I felt alone and abandoned.

The day Mom called me to talk with two detectives I had

reached the bottom of my despair. Suicidal thoughts plagued me. It was with a reluctant heart I entered the room where two men waited for me. My head was lowered as I sat on a dining-room chair. My hands were clasped so tightly they ached. Inside I screamed, "Don't they know each time I repeat my story, it's like being tortured?" My thoughts were interrupted when I heard a familiar voice say, "Karen, don't you remember me?"

When I looked up, I saw the deep blue eyes of my policeman friend, Bill. He gently placed his hands over mine and said, "This terrible thing was not your fault, it's okay to cry." Tears I'd kept locked up, escaped. Letting them flow began healing my hurting heart.

God's providence had been at work. Bill had been promoted to detective and assigned to my case. A few weeks later he was demoted back to police officer, because his supervisors felt he got too involved. Thank God he did. He became a surrogate dad to me.

Bill's friendship brought hope back into my life. He introduced me to his wife, Helen, who welcomed me. Their home was a safe harbor. On his days off or after work, Bill would stop by at my house and sit at our kitchen table, talking with me and Mom.

His unconditional love helped me to begin overcoming the trauma the rape had created. After the rapist was caught and sentenced, my friendship with Bill and Helen continued. Over the years we've shared graduations, weddings, births, funerals, and a blended mixture of tears and laughter. Our friendship has endured forty years.

What a difference it would make in the world if every individual reached out to help one hurting soul, and loved them with God's unconditional love—like Bill did for me.

—Karen Kosman

Me? Visit Shut-Ins!

Each time the Lord asked me to visit shut-ins, I just couldn't do it. I thought of the nursing home I'd visited a few years before with all those senile old people—some so repulsive, unkempt, and often using foul language—and the overwhelming odor!

"Oh, Lord," I prayed, "There must be some other way you could use me!" I even agreed to teach a first-grade Sunday school class to ease my conscience!

Unexpectedly, my friend Altene asked me if I would team up with her and visit shut-ins. In a weak (or maybe a strong) moment I said, "Yes."

Our first assignment was to visit an eighty-nine-year-old woman, Mrs. Dean, who lived at home. Her gracious manner showed obvious refinement. We noticed she had poor eyesight and she said, "I can only see colors if the light is just right."

I realized that the red roses I'd cut from my garden weren't the right gift, but Mrs. Dean accepted them gratefully. She enjoyed their fragrance for a moment, and with her touch method, found a vase and placed them in water.

She told us, "My days seem long since my son and daughter-in-law both work, but I'm not bored with life. I listen to Christian radio and keep up on the news. I praise the Lord for every new day and thank Him for my continued health." Her ears were her antennae to the outside world.

I was surprised when I thoroughly enjoyed visiting with her. Weekly we learned more of her amazing life—her move to Arizona as a young girl before it became a state. The pride in marrying a Christian man and rearing two healthy sons.

One day Mrs. Dean reminisced about her childhood home in a farming community in Ohio. She mentioned that her cousin was still editor of the weekly newspaper there. I'd heard of the town and tucked the fact away in my mind.

That summer on vacation, my husband and I came within a

few miles of her hometown and on impulse went to look up her cousin in the newspaper office. He was delighted to hear of her and sent a paper home with us as a token souvenir for her.

When I returned she could hardly believe I'd actually stopped in the town that was still "home" to her girlish heart. I read her a few excerpts from the paper and the editorial by her cousin. She beamed. Her pleasure gladdened my day and made our impulsive trip worthwhile.

On her ninetieth birthday, her family honored her with a surprise open house! I felt honored to be asked. She glowed and her acute ears recognized most of her guests by their voices.

One day, about a year later, as we concluded our visit, Mrs. Dean unburdened her heart, "I want to ask you to pray for my sons after I'm gone. They have become so caught up in making money that they have neglected the Lord they once loved." Her dim eyes filled with tears as she quoted Psalm 106:15, *And he gave them their request; but sent leanness into their soul.*

Altene and I prayed right then and promised we'd continue.

Some months later we received news that Mrs. Dean had suffered a stroke. Altene and I went to visit her in the nursing home, not knowing what to expect. The many distasteful things I disliked about nursing homes were still there—but now I didn't consider them. I was visiting a friend who might need us.

Mrs. Dean lay staring at the ceiling, unable to talk. I took her hand in mine but she didn't respond when I asked her to squeeze my hand. As we prepared to leave, I reminded her, "We won't forget our promise to pray for your sons."

It was then I felt the pressure on my hand. She did know! Then she smiled radiantly and spoke as if those unseeing eyes had glimpsed something beyond our sight, "Mine eyes have seen the glory of the coming of the Lord."

Is she seeing something beyond our human eyes? I pondered. I was sure she wasn't just quoting the line of the song by Julia Ward Howe.

Altene and I realized we would miss our long visits with Mrs.

Dean even though we now visited several others. She had become a dear friend those last four years.

A short time later her name flashed out from the obituary column. It seemed so curt and cold. Oh, how I wanted to rewrite it to read:

"Mrs. Dean, a lovely saint of the Lord, met her Master last Thursday. Now she can see the beautiful colors of heaven and was joined with her loved ones there. On earth she has left a prayer for her sons and their children and grandchildren."

I prayed. "Don't let me forget my promise. And thank you, Lord, for insisting that I visit shut-ins!"

—Mary Lou Klingler

God Needs To Prepare Us

Sometimes God needs to prepare us
  For duties down the road,
  So burdens that we carry now
  May seem a heavy load.

Hospitals used to frighten me
  —It was hard to even breathe—
  But Grandma was sick, so I went
  . . . But couldn't wait to leave.

It's my husband now, who's been sick
  But I'm no longer scared—
  For through the years God's been guiding
  —My heart He has prepared.

Now, as I walk within the halls
  That used to bring such fright,
  I see a lady in one room
  With hair of purest white . . .

Somehow I feel her sadness now,
  And her lonely sorrow:
  She wonders what her future holds . . .
  Or if she'll see tomorrow.

I turn and walk into her room
  —Praising God all the way—
  That He's prepared me through the years . . .
  To brighten up her day!

—Denise A. DeWald

Leave Me Some Dignity!

"Marjie, do you want your hair cut?" I asked. It didn't take Marjie long to think through the question before she blurted out a firm, "No!" To her, getting a haircut would only mean further humiliation to her already battered dignity; she had so little hair left, it didn't matter how it looked.

It was early afternoon and Tony, Marjie's husband, had just picked me up after work since my car was in the shop for repairs. He was planning dinner for the three of us. There hadn't been a chance to get together for weeks.

Now, standing in the doorway of the warm and elegant master bedroom, I gazed fondly at Marjie as she lay back against the quilted headboard. Marjie was my childhood friend, and she was dying of cancer. The rose-colored comforter was thrown back and a mound of white, spongy pillows held up her pale, balding head. Tufts of light brown fuzz stuck out in sparse patches all over her scalp. The memory of her thick, golden-brown braids bouncing off her back as we played when we were kids, filled me with pain.

Tony was sitting in the chair beside the bed. Usually easy going, he was now visibly agitated. He'd asked me to trim his wife's hair. But I noticed when he asked Marjie, "How about a haircut, sweetie?" she put her head down, frowned, drew her lips together in a tight pout, and shook her head vehemently.

I sensed the struggle going on inside my friend. Marjie wanted to please Tony; it was such a simple request. Yet, to her, most of her womanhood had already been stripped away; and now, she was fighting for this last sign of her femininity; the little bit of hair she had left.

Marjie had been diagnosed with cancer—malignant tumor on her thyroid—ten years earlier at the age of 50. After surgery, she continued to live a full and happy life.

However, two years later, breast cancer was detected and then three years ago malignant tumors were found in her brain. Reluctantly, she consented to chemotherapy. But recently, her doctors suggested that treatments be discontinued. The disease had progressed so far, that to continue invading her deteriorating body was senseless.

Tony had made the difficult decision to stop the treatment. A devoted family man, their only child away at college, he insisted he would give her full time care in their home. Little did he understand just what being a full time caregiver would mean.

Tony left the bedroom to start dinner in the kitchen. Meanwhile, I moved to the chair beside the bed. I reached over and took Marjie's hands in my own and asked, "Would you like me to fix your nails?" A small tear hung at the corner of Marjie's eye as she hesitantly replied, "Thank you."

I thought, "Thank You, God, for the chance to give back some of the love Marjie has given me over the years."

After we had dinner, Tony drove me home. His right hand made fluttering motions around his head, as he lamented, "If Marjie could only see how silly she looks with the pieces of hair sticking out from under the wig, she'd want her hair cut."

"Tony, even though Marjie's body is sick and helpless, there's a woman inside who's alive and alert," I explained. "She's always been a vivacious person, full of fun and laughter, impeccable in her taste in clothes and style. You know all about the weekly appointments at her hairdresser. Marjie has always taken pride in how she looks. Don't tear away the last shred of dignity she has left."

I continued, "She can't bathe, walk or dress herself. Little things, like having some hair on her head, having nicely trimmed nails, feeling clean and smelling pretty, are still important to Marjie. It makes her feel feminine and valuable . . . like the wife she still longs to be. Tony, have you considered bringing in someone to help you care for her?"

Tony thoughtfully listened as he guided the car along the darkened streets. Pulling alongside the curb in front of my house, Tony put the car in park and breathed a long, heavy sigh. "You've enlightened me on some things about Marjie. I just never thought about . . . well . . . her dignity. I'm doing all I know to do, taking care of the house and her needs the best way I know how. There just isn't time for much else. But I hear what you're saying. She needs more—little personal things I can't do for her.

"I need to put aside my fears and look for someone to help me. She needs a woman's touch to make her last days more comfortable and pleasant. She deserves to feel valuable, and to know she's as attractive to me as she's always been. I'll make some phone calls first thing in the morning."

I felt a peace flood my being as I silently prayed, "Thank You, Lord, for moving on Marjie's behalf; and for giving me the words to help Tony understand." I climbed out of the car and waved as he pulled away from the curb. Stepping over the damp grass, I started up the path to my house and smiled, "Marjie, it's going to be all right, God has everything under control!"

—Marilyn Krebs

Gifts On The First Day In May

The morning burst with energy, like new blossoms rising out of gray barren branches. The wind whipped my hair as I kneeled in the shadow of the old maple tree. The aroma of sweet and sour bark, and pine needles warmed to perfection, surged through me, while playing memories back like an old familiar song. I clipped forget-me-nots and pansies and piled them into a shallow box.

Back in the kitchen I arranged the delicate flowers in bright paper cups. When my children were young, we crafted many baskets to add to the ones they made at school. Years later, the grandchildren and I carried May baskets to the nursing home. Now all the children were older; some lived at quite a distance. But I carried on our ritual and looked forward to checking on my friends.

I arrived at the nursing home alone—feeling a little silly without a child in tow—but I soon forgot myself in the gracious response of the people.

One shriveled little lady said, "I remember when I took May baskets to my neighbors." The gentlemen gratefully accepted the addition to their lunch table. Some could not speak, but in their eyes I read a thousand thanks and saw a memory come to life.

I visited the rooms of those having lunch alone and shared a moment in the patchwork quilt of their lives. They grinned with pleasure as I admired their grandchildren's pictures and artwork.

I had promised to bring some of my poems to my friend who reads voraciously. "Come in," she called, showing me her new stuffed bear. "Buster plays a tune when I squeeze his ear. And he sleeps with me every night."

In the next room, an old timer in the valley shared his tales of fishing and hunting. "Those were the good old days," he commented with delight. "But today is okay too. I get a sunbath through this window every clear morning."

An old friend called out from her room. She was busily

counting hankies in her dresser drawer. I admired her hair ribbon and reminded her of the stamp collection she gave our son when he delivered newspapers to her years before. She paused and flashed a brilliant smile. "You know, it's been a good life. It's really been fun."

Another resident held up her orange terrycloth bear and explained, "When my granddaughter was eleven and had no money to buy me a Christmas gift, she made 'Teddy O' for me." She smiled and put him in my arms. "He was the first thing I packed when I left home to live here. I have a good room and I can watch the sunset coloring the clouds. I can even see the flag waving high above the Post Office."

In the next room, a lady thanked me for the basket. She held up a lacy white creation as she sat contentedly with oxygen tubes in her nose, a bow in her hair, and a crochet hook in her hands. "I'm making a tablecloth for my granddaughter," she explained, patting out the delicate pattern for me to see.

Another lady making scarves out of multicolored yarn scraps, proudly placed one of them in my hand. "When I first came here I cried a lot. Now I make scarves for the homeless."

In the dining room, a resident played a melody from the past and I brushed tears from one woman's wrinkled face.

"It's almost too beautiful, isn't it?" I asked, holding her hand.

Then I made my way through the patients in wheelchairs in the entryway. I hugged them and promised to come back soon as they pulled me down for another kiss.

I had ventured out to share some of the outdoors with those confined inside, and as always, I was the one blessed. I carried the memory of gentle faces and wise, sparkling eyes as I walked out into the sunshine.

I looked down and smiled. A stray forget-me-not was caught in my sweater. Love was caught in my throat.

—Doris Hays Toppen

Fifty-Two Steps

It was a dull morning, and I was walking in the yard when I saw Nancy, my next-door neighbor, on the way to her mailbox. I quickly stepped behind our shed. I hated hiding like this; but since we weren't on speaking terms, I had learned it was easier for both of us if we didn't run into each other very often.

I felt someone watching me and turned to find Jennifer, Nancy's little three-year-old, studying me curiously. I wanted to smile but didn't, fearing she wouldn't smile back. My heart ached! Jeni and I had always been so close.

How hard it must be for a child to understand hate. I could tell by her sad brown eyes and bewildered expression, she didn't understand at all.

The whole mess had started when someone told me some things Nancy had said about me and I'd gotten mad. I vowed never to speak to her again. I couldn't wait to lash out at her with my anger. But she never questioned my self-imposed distance.

Six months had passed. I began wondering who I was hurting more, Nancy or I? It had seemed so right at first. But I'd never taken the time to discuss the problem with her. Maybe she'd never said anything about me in the first place. I wanted to erase the entire incident.

I remembered how in happier days Nancy and I had laughed about the split rail fence I planned to put around my yard, how it would need a gate between her house and mine. The fence never materialized; instead a different kind of wall stood between us. This wall wasn't visible to anyone driving by, but Jeni knew it was there. I did too, and I was ashamed.

Nancy's stern voice calling Jeni home brought me back to the present and the pain. Tears brimmed my eyes as Jeni quickly darted away. I wanted to call her back, take her in my arms, and explain that my anger wasn't meant for her, just her mother. How proud I used to be when Jeni would run to me with outstretched arms whenever I came to visit. I wanted to march over to Nancy right then and angrily confront her. Instead, I walked disheartened into the house.

I loved God and prayed often about this misunderstanding. Yet I knew my relationship with Him was strained, because I couldn't pray for anyone or anything else. It was as if I were in the grip of something that paralyzed me from taking action.

Another six months passed, and I was really feeling miserable! How could I let this go on for so long? I called myself a Christian but didn't speak to my neighbor when we passed on the street. With each new day, I felt more like a hypocrite.

I can't count the times I prayed for God to lift me bodily from my kitchen into Nancy's house because I just couldn't seem to get there on my own. Of course, He never did! I knew His mysterious ways well enough to know that I must be willing to take that first step all on my own. Then, and only then, would He open the door of opportunity, prepare the path before me, and provide the much-needed strength.

Not long after that, as I was reading my Bible, I John 4:20 stood out as if they were the only words on the page. Through it, God told me, *If you say you love me, and hate your neighbor, you are a liar.* Me? Not love God! "I do love You, God. I'm not lying! Forgive me, Lord! I don't hate Nancy; You know that."

Yes, God knew that. He had known it for some time. Suddenly, I knew it too. But Nancy didn't. I had to tell her. I knew this was the time. Taking a deep breath, I started the seemingly endless walk toward my neighbor's home.

As I walked, I unconsciously counted my steps, twenty-one, twenty-two, twenty-three. I wondered what I would find at my journey's end. Acceptance or rejection? My heart raced and my mind ran wild. What if she slams the door in my face? I wouldn't blame her if she did.

My steps grew less deliberate as these recurring questions taunted me. I wanted to turn and run. There was no room for doubt. God was leading and I was following. I wouldn't turn back. My steps continued—fifty, fifty-one. I glanced up at Nancy's kitchen window, hoping she would be there doing dishes. She was, and as our eyes met, we both smiled.

That last step into her home was so easy to take. "Well, Nancy, I'm a year late, but I finally made it. Can you ever forgive me?" She took me in her arms, and I knew God's will had been done.

We never have discussed what was said, or who said it—there is no need. I hear Jeni's cheerful little voice yell, "Hi, Marcia!" as I walk through my yard. I am truly grateful.

—**Marcia Krugh Leaser**

7

Support

A friend loves at all times, and a brother is born for adversity.

Proverbs 17:17

"The God Is Faithful" Luncheon

My mastectomy was less than a week away. So much was going on in the roller coaster of my mind . . . including overwhelming gratitude that the Lord, in His mercy, had lead me to an ingenious reconstruction technique that would not only leave me whole after the cruel amputation of my breast, but console me with the fantasy I'd joked about since giving birth . . . a "tummy tuck."

Even so, the dread I felt because of what was ahead became a heavy weight. My dear friends, Ronnie, Keegan and Peggy, wanted to show me their love and encouragement by treating me to lunch; but I just wanted to stay home in my sweats. I called Ronnie and tried to make excuses. She said they were all looking forward to our lunch date and I wasn't going to back out. Determination is Ronnie's middle name, so I knew it was futile to argue. I reluctantly dragged myself to the mirror in an attempt to spiff myself up and summon a smile.

As Peggy drove us downtown, Ronnie slipped a tape into the cassette player, presenting me with a song. *He's Been Faithful to Me*, performed by the incredible Damaris Carbaugh, filled the car with music. It was clear that this song had profound meaning to her and was a special gift of love from her heart to mine. I thanked her, but all I could feel was an overwhelming sadness. As tears started to roll down my cheeks, Keegan, sitting next to me, reached over and held my hand.

We browsed in a little boutique, then entered the restaurant. As we were escorted to our table I was astounded to discover about a dozen of my friends. I stood there stunned while they pinned a beautiful corsage on me and presented me with a gift, a guest book. Written on the first page was, "The God is Faithful Luncheon, in Honor of Sherry Lynn." Inside, each one of them had expressed their love to me, along with words of encouragement and scripture. Ronnie explained, "Whoever comes to the hospital while you're in surgery or visits while you recuperate is supposed to write you a note."

Lynn, my frequent partner in lunacy, presented me a special "hospital ensemble," a truly *ugly* pink nightgown and a trashy feather boa. She said, "I know that hot pink clashes with your red hair, but never fear for I have solved that problem!" Then she pulled out a very bouffant, very long, platinum blonde wig.

Next, she presented me with a pair of very dainty and stylish cow slippers, complete with their tongues hanging out on the floor. An impressive ensemble! I knew the other patients would be green, er . . . hot pink with envy! Of course, if I had chosen to wear that lovely ensemble at the hospital, the staff might have insisted that I add one of their "captivating" white jackets. (You know . . . the one that wraps your arms snugly around your waist and ties in the back!) My delightful friends plopped the wig on top of my head, held up the nighty and feather boa, and took pictures. I'm quite sure I was stunning, I know I was stunned.

We laughed throughout the luncheon. The servers at the restaurant, as well as other diners, got involved . . . offering to take pictures for us, laughing, admiring my outfit. A group of businessmen stopped by our table on their way out. One of them put his hand on my shoulder and told me he had been watching our party and couldn't figure out if my friends REALLY liked me or REALLY hated me! Then he smiled, winked, patted my shoulder and said, "Nice outfit!"

Those around us affected by our luncheon probably thought it was my birthday. I'm sure they would have been shocked to know that I had cancer, and my friends wanted to brighten my day with an encouragement luncheon!

We had a wonderful time as I basked in the love and support that was poured out on me on a day that had started out so low. The memory of it still touches me. Their gift filled my joy tank to overflowing—when it had started out so empty! On that day, the Lord used my friends to turn my *mourning into dancing* (Psalm 30:11)! When I left the restaurant my heart danced from the warmth of their love.

When my husband, Jerry, came home from work, I was wearing the ensemble, wig and all, for the full effect. He commented, as he had many times before, that life with me is never boring. He, too, was touched and very grateful for the gift of love and encouragement given to me on that snowy afternoon.

I thanked the Lord that night for the way He turned a melancholy morning into a heartwarming afternoon of affection and affirmation. My friends' compassion and thoughtfulness not only ministered to me but affected those around us. The people in the restaurant were aware that there was something special about that luncheon and wanted to be a part of it. They never knew that they had witnessed a "divine" lunch date . . . "The God Is Faithful" Luncheon.

—**Sherry Karuza Waldrip**

Blessings In Disguise

So many blessings are disguised
  By pain and trials sore—
We cannot see the end result
Or what God has in store.

For often through our suffering
We come to know God's love,
And feel the peace He showers down
From Heaven up above.

And did you ever stop to think
Of how much you've grown?
For in all that you have gone through,
You were never alone.

God held your hand along the way—
Though you were not aware—
He helped you lift each heavy cross,
And every burden bear.

Just take some time to reflect
On what He's brought you through—
He'll never leave you on your own,
No matter what you do.

So thank Him now on bended knee for
Your blessings in disguise:
Your character's been strengthened, friend—
More than you realize.

—Denise A. DeWald

Go With God

Christine was an older woman who had cancer throughout her body. I was the nurse in charge of her for that evening shift and it was obvious that she wasn't going to last the night.

"I'm so scared. Please don't leave me alone," she pleaded, grabbing my arm.

I had eight other patients to care for but I gave her as much attention as I could during the shift.

Christine's biggest fear seemed to be that she wouldn't get to see her husband one more time. He was trying to get there. The nurses had called and told him the end was near, but he was still several hours away on a business trip. No one had expected her health to decline so fast.

"I'm so scared. *Please* don't leave me alone," she pleaded again.

"Christine, I get off duty in twenty minutes, but I have to chart now. When I'm off, I'll sit with you a while before I go home. I'll also tell the night nurse how afraid you are. Okay?"

She didn't look like it was okay, but she agreed. I turned her on her side, padded her with pillows, and went about my final charting. In my report, I told the nurse how scared Christine was, then clocked out and went back to her room. Her husband was still about two hours away. I couldn't stay that long because my husband also worked there and he'd be ready to leave in another half hour, but I figured I would give her what comfort I could. That also gave her nurse a chance to get vital signs taken on her other patients.

Christine wanted to sit up, so I helped her, then, breaking hospital rules since I was now off duty, I sat beside her and held her close. "Are you afraid of dying?" I asked her.

"Yes. I wish I knew what it will be like. What if I die before my husband gets here?" I could tell by her eyes she was in a lot of pain, but I didn't know how much was physical and how much emotional. "I don't want to die alone. Please stay with me." I had a knot in the middle of my chest. How could I help her?

I had looked at her chart. She was a Catholic and had already received last rights. I asked, "Do you know Jesus?"

"Yes."

"He's here with you even when no one else is."

"Oh! I forgot. I'm still so afraid, though."

"His angels are always around us, even though we can't see them. God promises He'll never leave us or forsake us." I could tell she was starting to calm down. Then I asked her if she'd like us to pray together and she said yes.

I don't remember all of the prayer, but I know we prayed that she would have peace and joy as she went to be with our Lord. Then we prayed that her husband would arrive in time for them to have time together.

Then I had to leave to meet my husband. It was so hard to leave, but she had a look of peace on her face now. I assured her that I would tell her nurse I was leaving and that I would continue to pray for her.

The next day, when I returned to work, I learned that Christine's husband arrived about half an hour before she went to be with our Lord. He was holding her as she died in peace. God had answered our prayers.

This was the first time I realized that I could get blessed during the loss of a patient. I knew God was with her and, if He was with her, He is always with me. *Even though I walk through the valley of the shadow of death, I will fear no evil, for you are with me;* . . . Psalm 23:4.

—Nancy E. Peterson

No Tears Left

Ole was past 90. His mind was still clear; but his sight, hearing and locomotion were impaired. For the last few years he'd been living at a nursing home. He was in the lobby when I visited him shortly after his sister's death.

When I expressed sympathy for his grief, Ole said, "I can't cry. I got no tears left. My parents, my wife, my daughter and grandson, my brother and now my sister. All gone.

"Except for my mother, they all died younger than I am now. And I'm still here." He stared at his scarred, gnarled hands. I could find no response to the raw pain he had exposed before he spoke again.

"I don't know how long I have to stay here. But I know that when Jesus Christ comes back, the ones who know him will rise up and go with him. For the others, it will be too late."

Ole couldn't hear another fellow resident express agreement from her wheelchair.

"Now I can't do anything but wait for Jesus to take me. I got no more tears in me."

Ole's dry-eyed grief wrung my heart. I touched his hands—their tremor was very strong—and sat with him in silence, praying he would be given the release of tears.

The following day, Ole's sons helped him into the church early for his sister's funeral. He sat alone in the pew, trembling from the effort of the walk, while his sons went downstairs where the family was gathering. One of his granddaughters, about five years old, went up and silently laid her blond head on his shoulder. Ole's arm curved around her. Then his shoulders shook and an off-white handkerchief came out.

I whispered thanks for answered prayer in the tender, wordless wisdom of a young child and the blessing of tears.

—Florence Ferrier

Let The Combines Roll

It was graduation night, and the festive mood seemed to fill the air. Becky had left her friends in town to return home to her parents' farm. Her mind was filled with wild anticipation, as she left her friends to the excitement of their own dreams.

Becky Adams had much on her mind as she drove down the dark country roads. Wheat harvest was near and Dad had gotten all of his equipment ready early in the rainy season so he could take some time off for all of the events surrounding his only child's graduation.

Suddenly, cresting a hill, bright on-coming lights blinded Becky, and her right tires went off the edge of the black top road. All the measurements and markings by the Highway Patrol indicated that she had struggled hard to gain control of her car before careening down the embankment. She had died instantly, according to the coroner's report. She was already dead before the overturned vehicle caught fire and exploded.

Dora and John Adams were in a state of disbelief as the young County Sheriff's deputy did his best to console them. Becky had been the light of her parent's lives for eighteen years. Before Becky's arrival, they had been married fifteen years and had given up hope of having a child. But when Dora became pregnant at age 37, their lives were drastically changed.

Now, their lives would never again be the same because of their great loss. Dora wondered how she and John had lived so happily all those years alone, before Becky. Now, how would they ever fill their hearts and days? There was plenty of work to do, but no heart left to do it. Like all struggling small farmers, they had experienced hard times. They were of pioneer stock and not prone to self-pity or quitting easily. But this time they faced a mountain, unlike any they had ever faced. They did not know how to get up and start moving. Love and purpose seemed to have died and they wondered if they would ever experience a reason for living again.

John knew the wheat was about to ruin in the field. He also knew that the bank loan had to be paid out of this year's wheat crop, but he had been too immobilized by pain to care or reason that they could lose their farm.

After the exhaustion of the funeral, they both fell tearfully into a deep sleep.

The sun had barely started to climb in the Eastern sky, when an unexpected noise awakened them. They looked at each as if they'd been dreaming the same dream and went to the bedroom window.

They could hardly believe their eyes but their ears had not lied to them. Combine after combine was coming up the drive and entering their fields like a procession of toys come to life at night in a nursery. Rows of wheat began to disappear rapidly. John's eyes manned the horizon and he said to Dora, "Every combine in the county must be here."

Suddenly, Dora noticed movement in their garden, just below their bedroom window. A group of women in the shadowy morning light were working quickly; weeding, cultivating, staking and watering. "Look down there, John; they have it nearly back in shape already." Dora wondered how long they had been working quietly beneath her window.

Smiles crept across John and Dora's faces. Something they had not thought they would ever see again. John wrapped his arms around Dora. With smiles on their faces and tears in their eyes, they felt a sense of life in their souls. They dressed quickly. Dora ran downstairs to put on coffee before going out to greet the women in her garden.

The moment lights had gone on in the Adam's house, a combine had left the field and moved toward the house. Dan Jackson, a neighbor and friend, stopped the large machine in the driveway. He yelled to John as he stood on the porch quickly hooking the straps of his bib overalls, "Come on aboard, John, we've wheat to harvest before breakfast." Again a smile crossed John's face. It felt good. He climbed up in the cab beside Dan.

"No need to say nothing, John," Dan explained. "We aren't Becky, but we're all family around here and now we're all you've got." He reached over and squeezed John's shoulder, and as men will do, they went right into talk about the equipment, the weather and the harvest.

The "women of the morning hour," as Dora quickly named them, followed her into the house with groceries they had brought for a big breakfast. Each seemed to find a comfortable place either mixing biscuits or sipping coffee and visiting. Tears of joy streamed down Dora's face as she turned to them and said, "You've no idea how good all of this noise sounds. I think all of the quiet of losing a teenager was just about to kill us both. But none of you girls ever did grow up and you sound almost as good as my Becky. Thank you. You see, John and I forgot that when God closes a door, he always opens a window. Today we've learned that there's more than one way to fill an empty hole, and more than one kind of love to be cherished."

—Cheryl L. Williams

8

Divorce

Those who sow in tears will reap with songs of joy. He who goes out weeping, carrying seed to sow, will return with songs of joy, carrying sheaves with him.

Psalm 126:5-6

Perfect Shells And Broken Pieces

I walked along the beach early one autumn morning, hoping to find shells for my collection. The summer tourists had gone home, and the kids had returned to school. The beach was deserted, except for an elderly couple walking hand-in-hand and a man scavenging with a metal detector. I seemed to be the only person searching for shells.

However, everywhere I looked I saw broken pieces. I kicked at the sand in frustration. The broken shells reminded me of the fragmented pieces my life had become with the breakup of my marriage.

The wind whipped my hair and sent a chill down my back. I pulled my sweatshirt around me and kept walking. Somehow, I hoped my brisk pace would help me to leave my problems behind to be swept out with the tide. Instead, the waves kept bringing in more and more broken shells.

I stopped for a moment and cried out, "Where are you, Lord? What plan do you have for the broken pieces of my life?"

I resumed walking, trying to gain some perspective on my situation. What had happened to my perfect little family of four? Like the shells, my hopes and dreams for the future had been dashed on the rocks.

God seemed silent. Yet, I sensed the fault was mine, not His. I wasn't seeking His guidance so much as I was venting my anger by shouting.

Another wave surged on the shore, and I continued my search. To my surprise, this one brought in a beautiful whole shell. Scooping it up in my hand, I turned it over and noticed how perfectly God had formed it. In the midst of all this broken-ness was wholeness.

Perhaps God would make me whole, too. However, I needed to do my part. Instead of dwelling on my problems and unmet expectations, I needed to plan for the future. I no longer had a husband, but I did have two wonderful teenage boys. The three of us were still a family.

We could build on what we have. We could love and encourage each other. We could laugh and plan inexpensive outings together. We could look to the future, knowing God would guide our path if only we allowed Him.

Perhaps, if I stopped shouting at God, I would be able to hear Him speak to me. Once again, I looked down at the perfect shell in my hand and smiled. Had God already spoken?

—Susan Titus Osborn

A Cry In The Night

"Welcome aboard Flight 703, departing Orange County to San Jose." The attendant's words barely registered as I stared ahead. My three-year old daughter was strapped tightly in the seat next to me while I held my six-month old son against me.

Slumping in my seat, I thought, *I haven't slept for 36 hours. Why won't my eyes shut?* Squeezing them, the sudden pressure of my swollen lids reminded me of the frequent outbursts of tears over the past few weeks. My body ached, my head throbbed, and I fought nausea.

This isn't happening to me . . . what will my parents think when I tell them? The truth was that my husband wasn't happy in our marriage and wanted distance rather than confrontation to decide its value. *I bet being in the house alone will show him how much he wants and needs his family. When I return home, we'll start a new life together.* I held those comforting thoughts as we began to taxi the runway.

The engine roared louder. My baby sucked his bottle persistently while my daughter squeezed my limp hand, grinning with excitement. I forced a smile for her.

As the plane took flight, I was flooded with fear. *Someone is missing! Where is my husband?* I felt like standing in the aisle, screaming, "Help! I'm all alone!"

"Look at the lights, Mommy!"

I muttered, "Oh, pretty." The bottle was empty and my son needed attention.

"Let's sing a song, Mommy," my daughter begged. In a joyful high-pitched voice, she began, "Jesus loves me, this I know, for the Bible tells me so . . ."

As if they were stones, I began throwing words at God. "You love me, huh? You've caused me to hurt like this—is that love? What about this morning?"

Had I been abandoned only this morning? The past few weeks my husband had grown very distant. Something lay between us but it remained a complete mystery to me. Day after day of rejection brought confusion, despair, and sleeplessness. Dropping my head on the headrest, I realized that for the first time in almost fourteen years I didn't know where my husband was. Earlier this morning, I had offered to take the children to my parents so he could have some time and space to "sort things out." Since he had left for the day he didn't even know if I had actually gone to my parents. *Did he even care?*

Surely he will call my parents' house when he finds us gone. He'll want to know if we have arrived safely. I felt relief at the thought that, after so many years together. I could count on certain things.

Suddenly I felt a weight of responsibility I'd never known. *I'm all alone! I'll have to make every decision alone. He won't even be at the airport to help carry the suitcases!*

Little was said when I arrived at my parents' home and after settling the children for bed, I went directly to mine. But I couldn't sleep. My husband's actions were so unlike the man with whom I had spent half my life. *What's to become of my future?* I wondered. It felt like my whole world was falling apart.

I shook my fist at the ceiling and reminded God of the injustice of my situation. Though I didn't feel any of His love at that moment, I did remember a verse that said, *I will never leave you or forsake you* (Hebrews 13:5). *Maybe this is the time to take God at His word. Can I believe God's love will be so trustworthy that He will stand with me, no matter what happens in my life?*

I sobbed, "Oh God, whatever You want from me, You've got it. Help me! Help me sleep, think, care for my kids, make the right choices . . . follow You. I have nothing to offer You—except me. I feel so weak, scared, unsure, rejected, unloved. Go ahead and take me Lord, it seems no one else wants me anyway."

The phone never rang. My pillow was drenched. My eyes stung, but I drifted off to sleep, a solid sleep that dreamed of having an unshakable faith to call my own.

Months later, while sipping coffee with a friend, she asked,

"Where in the world does your joy come from in the midst of such pain?"

As I answered, I had the assurance that my dream had become a reality. I blurted, "It's Jesus! He's become everything to me! Any joy you see is the result of His peace. Peace, because I know God is faithful in spite of so many others being unfaithful!"

Hesitating she countered, "But, how do you ever go about trusting someone you can't even see?"

Her question interrupted my reflection of what a nightmare the past few months would have been, had I not chosen to trust God and His promises. I was mindful that God is not threatened by my honest questions, weak faith, or accusations. He merely loves me just as He promised and has brought wholeness to my broken life.

"You can see Him! He's reflected in nature . . . in people . . . in people who have no logical reason to be joyful."

As I continue waiting to see the final direction of my marriage I may cry a thousand more tears. The pain of my first plane ride might come again, but never—never again will I be alone.

—Jan Northington

A Table Full Of Single Socks
And How I Dealt With It

The hour was late. I had just received my second wind for the evening, enabling me to tackle the housework, my second full-time job. I am a single mother of two small boys, and after putting in eight hours at the office, coming home and feeding two hungry kids, bathing and putting them to bed, I usually don't have the energy to plunge into endless household chores. However, over the weekend, the kids and I spent a few hours in their bedroom setting things straight and retrieving dirty laundry from unimaginable hiding places. Now, I was finally finishing up the last of the laundry.

I had been astounded at how creative my children were in their messiness. I had asked Sammy, my four year old, how this one particular sock managed to be perched over the curtain rod. As Sammy is only three feet tall, I felt that this was a fair enough question. He answered me quite cleverly, "Mommy, I kicked it off!" I could kick until the cows come home but my socks will never be "kicked off" my feet. This must be some new skill Sammy has developed on his own.

As I sorted and folded their laundry, I set aside the task of matching the striped crew socks for last, thinking "Aha! Now I'll find all those missing socks." Instead, I ended up having more stray socks than when I started—in fact, more than a dozen!

Single socks irritate me. Some folks can pair them up with another sock the same size and basic color and not be bothered by it. Not me. If the stripes at the top of the socks do not match, that sock is history. *This is too much to handle at midnight*, I lamented. *Should I just go ahead and pair them up regardless of the stripes? Or should I wait until the next sock-hunting expedition in hopes of finding the correct mate? No one will know that the two socks aren't the original pairing—unless it's a hot day and the kids decide to wear shorts!*

Suddenly the hilarity of my obsession struck me and I laughed until I cried. My dogs stared at me, riveted, certain that I had, indeed, finally gone mad. As the hour was late, I elected to go to bed and sleep on it, all the while thinking that surely, there was a lesson to be learned from the socks.

The next morning the single socks were still on the kitchen table exactly as I'd left them the night before. They hadn't made their escapes as their mates had earlier. They lay there, passive; a mockery to my belief that everything must have a mate.

And then it hit me: the lesson from the socks!

I had once been part of a "pair of socks" bundled away neatly in the drawer of life. Everywhere I went I had a mate. Granted, sometimes my mate bore a hole in his head but nevertheless, I had a mate. At every social function, we were together; every church party, we were together; school functions for the kids—you got it—we were together, and we appeared to be a nice pair of socks. But now, I am no longer married, a single sock out of kilter with the rest of the socks. Although I still have a lot of use left in me, I've been sidelined to the kitchen table of life waiting for a mate before I can feel "useful" in society again.

I realized I had two choices. First, I'm pretty sure that if I tried hard enough I could find another sidelined sock of a soul willing to become a pair. Imperfect matches are out there everywhere. I'm sure that with two of us working together, we could cover up our mismatched stripes long enough so that no one could see the difference. No one but me, of course, but more importantly, God would know. My second choice was to wait until the Lord brings the perfect sock, uh mate, into my life, creating a stylish yet comfortable pair. I elected the latter choice but decided that I could still be a useful sock.

There are lots of things single socks can do. Dust, for one thing; they can also be useful in first aid as bandages, or perhaps provide an afternoon puppet show for gullible toddlers. The options are endless.

And in the meantime, as long as I leave the decision about my singleness up to the Lord, I won't be stuck with a "heel." But for now, perhaps I'll just go barefoot and bypass all this trauma!

—Jeri Chrysong

A Thousand Ways

On a hot summer day in July, 1987, I stood in the Standard Publishing Booth on the floor of the Christian Booksellers Convention in Anaheim, California. As I shook hands with bookstore owners, I appeared confident on the outside with the excitement of having my first book, *Parables for Young Teens*, published. Yet, I hurt on the inside. My marriage of twenty-two years was about to end.

Questions unrelated to the convention floor excitement raced through my mind. Could I make a living writing books? How could I help support my two college-age sons? How would I ever pick up the pieces of my life again?

Six months later, and unknown to me, with heavy snow falling outside his parents' home in Boise, Idaho, Dick Osborn sat quietly in his room. After he had gone through his divorce, he spent a couple of years living with his parents in Boise. During the winter, he spent a lot of time reading an old, tattered Bible. One night while lying on his bed, one verse literally jumped out at him: *We toss the coin, but it is the Lord who controls the decision* (Proverbs 16:33 TLB).

While reading, he was also thinking about Sandy, a girl he had been dating in California. When he saw that verse, he wondered if he would eventually marry Sandy. He reached in his pocket for a quarter and flipped it up in the air, saying, "OK, Lord, are Sandy and I ever going to marry? If the coin comes down heads, we will, and if it comes down tails, we won't." The coin landed with the "tails" side up.

Glancing around the room, Dick's gaze fell on a *Lookout* magazine, lying upside down on the rug. On the back was an advertisement for *Parables for Young Teens*. Dick stared at the magazine and seeing my name pleaded, "Lord, who am I going to marry—Susan F. Titus?" Again, he flipped his coin up in the air, but this time it came down "heads."

"Lord, you're not listening to me. I don't know anyone named Susan Titus. I don't even know what state she lives in. How could I possibly marry her?" Soon he forgot the entire incident.

In time, Dick came back to California and joined the Single Parent Fellowship group at my church. He became acquainted with my best friend, Lucille, who worked for me part-time. One night Lucille said, "Dick, I want you to meet my boss, Susan."

As time progressed, Dick sat with Lucille and me at many SPF functions. One evening he asked me out, but I was dating someone else at the time, so I declined his invitation to a baseball game. He replied, "If you ever change your mind, let me know."

For months, his words circled in my mind. After I broke up with the man I was dating, I started hinting that I'd like to go out with Dick. However, he didn't take the hint. Finally, one Sunday while we were walking to the parking lot after church, I said, "Remember what you said about me telling you if I ever wanted to go out with you?"

He replied, "Yeah!"

"Well, I'd like to."

We had lunch the following Wednesday, and in that short hour, I began to realize how much we had in common. On Valentine's Day of 1992, while on an SPF skiing trip to Mammoth Mountain, we became engaged. He bought me a dozen long-stemmed red roses and proposed in front of 50 of our church friends. A fire crackled in the fireplace, and snow gently covered the landscape, providing a perfect backdrop.

Shortly thereafter, my son Rich was planning an extensive six-month tour overseas with the Beachboys, for whom he was the sound engineer and keyboard technician. He didn't want to pay rent for that time, so he made arrangements to store most of his stuff at my house.

While Dick was carrying some of Rich's boxes upstairs to his old bedroom, Dick noticed a framed book cover on the hall wall. He turned pale, and his mouth fell open. "Did you write that book?" he asked incredibly.

"Yes, why else would I have it hanging on my wall? *Parables for*

Young Teens was my first book," I said, noticing his strange reaction.

Later on our honeymoon in the Caribbean, Dick told me the story of how he had flipped a coin on a cold night in Boise, Idaho, over five years before. Then he said, "Don't tell anyone. They'll never believe it!"

—Susan Titus Osborn

Hash By Candlelight

We had been deeply wounded and joy seemed to have disappeared when Libby's father left us for a new life. All the members of the family were confused and devastated. Her older sister married young and left home. Her teen-age brother was in a boys' school where he could find guidance and healing. Only a few months before, we had been a family of five around our table, but now there was only Libby and me.

"You can't come in yet, Mother," nine-year-old Libby called through the locked front door. "I'll be ready in a minute." I could hear our little Chihuahua barking and some movement in the house. I had just returned from work and stood waiting, somewhat impatiently, my arms loaded with school books, until she finally let me inside.

Then I saw the table covered with a lace cloth and two lighted candles. "I made dinner for us, Mother. For a surprise for you."

I took off my coat, laid down my load of books and quieted Candy, our noisy little dog. I sat down at the head of the table set for two, and Libby placed a bowl in front of me.

"I only could make a can of hash, Mother. I didn't know how to make anything else. But we like hash, don't we?"

I assured her it was one of my favorite dishes. We bowed our heads and gave thanks to God for his goodness to us—and I fervently thanked God for my wonderful little girl.

We ate hash and catsup by candlelight, and it tasted like ambrosia! We weren't being nourished by hash alone, though. We were both being strengthened by love, courage and determination.

We tried to keep a family spirit and started several new customs, such as decorating our home every month for the season or a holiday. If there were no special day that month, we thought of something we could celebrate with small decorations and cheer.

It took effort, imagination and courage to try from day to day to rebuild a home out of the hurt, but we kept on trying. Libby was showing that same spirit when she served us hash by candlelight. Although only two of us, instead of five, sat at that festive table, love was there.

As time went on, we realized that God was with us all the time, guiding and gently healing the raw hurts. Libby grew up into a fine woman at whose table I have had many excellent meals.

But in my heart, the best meal of all was the one she prepared for me the night we had hash, love and courage by candlelight.

—Venus E. Bardanouve

The Proverbs 31 Woman

I've been divorced seven years. Christian society has insinuated that because I am divorced, I cannot be a Godly woman. This is strange thinking as my experience has been that my faith has increased a thousandfold since my marriage and subsequent divorce. I have learned and experienced God's attributes of mercy, love, and forgiveness. Therefore, I have reached the conclusion that I, along with thousands of other Christian divorced women, am a Godly woman, a somewhat modified Proverbs 31 Woman.

The Godly Divorcee.

An excellent woman, who can find? For her worth is far above jewels.

The hearts of her children trust in her and are confident they will be taken care of.

She strives to do her best, in spite of her singleness and resulting lack of on-hand assistance, all the days of her life.

She seeks bargains in thrift shops and gladly accepts hand-me-downs, making the necessary repairs in magical delight at the newly renovated classic styles.

She's crafty in the kitchen creating "surprise" meals from leftovers hidden in foreign plastic containers.

She rises while it is still night (after retiring only a few hours earlier) to turn on the crock pot for her family's dinner, not forgetting a handout for the faithful family dog who rises with her.

She considers a house and knows she can't afford it—yet. From her earnings, she sets aside a portion for her dreams, and shops with coupons at the local market.

Her faith is her strength and makes her mighty. She works out spiritually and mentally . . . and even physically when she has the time (and energy).

She stretches her income and watches her savings account

grow. Her bills are paid and utilities never turned off for non-payment.

She extends her hand to newer, heartbroken single moms embarking on her same, strange new lifestyle.

She's not afraid of cold weather because she knows, in faith, that somewhere in those large bags of hand-me-downs, someone included a coat for her children.

She is a creative dresser, powerfully so, and puts together many colorful get-ups.

Her husband is the Lord; and she boasts in Him.

She is gaining a reputation as the woman who "does it all."

Her children increase in wisdom and stature and are highly regarded by their educators.

She wears her newly-acquired strength and dignity like a cloak, and she now smiles at her future.

She comes together with other single moms and shares wisdom, tips, insights, and tidbits.

For the most part, her tongue is kind, except when periods of exhaustion and sleep deprivation bring her down.

She does her best with the housework as she rarely has an idle moment, and is creative in hiding dirty dishes when unexpected visitors pop in.

Her children love her and, with age, appreciate her efforts and sacrifices, and say with pride, "Many moms have fancy clothes and drive vans or really hot cars, but only you can build a bunk-bed with a screwdriver as your only tool."

Charm is deceitful and beauty is a waste of time.

But any woman who loves and honors the Lord, she shall be praised.

—Jeri Chrysong

9

Coping

*You will keep in perfect peace him whose mind is steadfast,
because he trusts in you.*

Isaiah 26:3

Waiting Had A Purpose

I can finally call him Father,
I can look into his face.
The former fear that gripped my soul
is gone without a trace.

I can rest in him and find the joy
he's longed for me to hold.
It's only been through waiting
That his plans he could unfold.

I wandered and I wallowed,
I wept from deep inside.
The waiting had a purpose, Lord,
It taught me to abide.

I wondered and I wrestled,
I whined before I knew.
The waiting had a purpose, Lord,
It brought me home to you.

At home with you, a peaceful place,
To abandon is so sweet.
My one and only longing
is the day that we shall meet.
To see your face, my precious Lord,
To worship at your feet,
The day is not far off,
When my joy will be complete.

I can finally call you Daddy—
As I've longed for years to do.
The waiting had a purpose, Lord,
The purpose was in you.

—Jan Frank

Playing By The Rules

Ed Harrell, a former trustee of the Moody Bible Institute, served in World War II as a Marine. Near the close of the war he was assigned with just a few other Marines to a highly-classified task. The assignment was so classified that they were not told its purpose or given more than a brief explanation of what they were to do. They were to proceed to San Francisco, where they would pick up a large crate that had been sent to San Francisco from Nevada. They were to guarantee that that crate was aboard the USS *Indianapolis* when it sailed from port and to stand watch over that cargo until it was dropped off at a small island in the Pacific. Obedient, but totally unaware of the purpose of the mission, the men delivered their assigned cargo to the Pacific island and remained aboard the *Indianapolis* as it set sail for the Philippines. So confidential was their mission that when the ship left the island for the Philippines its departure was unannounced and its ultimate port of arrival not made known to the men.

In transit from that island the USS *Indianapolis* was hit by three successive Japanese torpedoes. In a brief time the ship went down, leaving those who had survived the attack floating in life jackets in the ocean. No one in the outside world knew that they were there or that their ship had sunk.

For four and a-half days Ed Harrell floated in his life jacket in the Pacific. He started in a group of eighty, who made a large circle arm and arm in the ocean, encouraging each other and hoping that someone would see them and rescue them. After two days that group of eighty had dwindled to seventeen. The rest had broken away from the group and been attacked by sharks, or they had died as a consequence of drinking salt water from the ocean, creating a chemical imbalance in their bodies that brought on disorientation, hallucinations, and eventually death, as they disappeared beneath the waves.

Miraculously, after four days the group—now numbering

five—was noticed by a pilot flying at three thousand feet over the ocean. An oil slick on one of their now soggy, only partially supportive life jackets had reflected a flash of sunlight that caught the eye of the pilot, who was part of a sub-sweeping operation.

Three days after their departure from that tiny Pacific island the atom bomb was dropped on Hiroshima and Nagasaki, ending the war and saving an estimated hundreds of thousands of lives that would have been lost in a prolonged land war in the Japanese theater.

Parts to those bombs had been in the crate they had delivered. I asked Ed how he could possibly have resisted drinking water from the ocean all those days. His reply was simple. In his training as a Marine he had been drilled time and time again on the dangers of drinking salt water should he ever be marooned in the ocean. His training demanded that men stranded in the ocean should always stay together and never drink the water, regardless of how bad it got. Ed's commitment to stick to the rules no matter how critical the situation brought him through the crisis successfully.

Our success in the midst of suffering demands a response not unlike Ed's. God often assigns us to circumstances we don't understand or places us in situations about which we know little. Yet, in the midst of those divinely-classified encounters, He asks of us simply to trust Him and obey. When in the process we are torpedoed by unexpected crises, it is paramount that regardless of how we feel, or how deeply we are tempted to do otherwise, we respond according to the biblical principles, that will ultimately bring us through. As tough as it seems, stalwart submission to Biblical patterns of response is the key to success.

—Joseph M. Stowell

Alone On Saturday Night

One Wednesday, while sitting in my office, I realized that I had no plans for the coming weekend. It was like a panic attack, and my immediate reaction was to reach for the phone and start calling a few friends to make some plans. As I dialed the first number, that inner voice I was learning to hear said so clearly, "Can't you trust Me? Don't you know I am God of the weekends, too?"

I put the phone down and gulped. When the Spirit of God speaks to you so directly, you're pinned against the wall, and it wasn't comfortable right at that moment. *God of the weekends, too,* I thought. *Oh, sure, but I still don't want to be alone on Saturday night.* After a few minutes of vacillation, I said, "Okay, Lord, I'll not make any plans for this weekend, and I'll plan time with You for Saturday night. I'll prove that You are God of the weekends."

Things went great that weekend, and I accomplished a lot. I had planned to do some good reading Saturday evening and spend some of that time in prayer. No problem, until about 9:00 p.m. Then panic started to hit again. *I'm alone on Saturday evening. What's wrong with me?* There was that attitude creeping back into my thinking, and no wonder. It had been there for years, so cleaning it out was bound to take a bit of time.

What did I do? I just told the Lord how I felt. I cried, "Help," and He rescued me. Have you learned to yell for help to the Lord at those panic moments?

—**Mary Whelchel**

Lord, How Can I Help Them?

I desperately needed to understand Jennifer's grief. There appeared to be no end to her crying. The way she secluded herself in her room deeply concerned me.

"How can I reach her?" I thought. "Tom passed away months ago, yet Jennifer seems the hardest to console."

Knocking on Jennifer's door, I prayed that I might be able to unlock some secret hidden deep within her. Although I knew the pain and inner struggle of my own grief, the grief of a nine-year-old child baffled me.

Jennifer's soft, timid voice responded, "What do you want, Mom?"

I leaned my head against the door and answered, "Please let me come in. We need to talk. I think it will help if we share some feelings with each other."

My stomach tightened and lumps formed in my throat as she slowly opened the door and climbed onto her bed. I wanted to ask the right questions. But most of all, I wanted to hear the right answers.

Clearing my throat, I tried to act brave. "Jennifer, I understand that you miss Daddy a lot. I want to help you with your hurt, but I don't know how. Please help me understand."

Jennifer sat motionless, playing with a small string in her hand. Tears began to well up in her eyes but words found no exit.

Touching Jennifer's hand, I calmly responded, "Please tell me what you're thinking. I need to know what hurts you most."

The quietness of the moment seemed like an hour. *Why wouldn't she speak?*

Finally, Jennifer looked up. My heart ached for her as I watched the tears stream down her face.

"Mommy, God took the wrong parent," Jennifer sobbed. With that she returned to her pensive position, shutting herself off again.

Stunned, I gave her a kiss on the cheek and quietly dismissed myself from her room. I didn't know whether to scream or sob hysterically. The hurt inside cut at my heart as I replayed the words in my mind, "Mommy, God took the wrong parent."

Tom's death had seared all of our hearts. I tried to cope by staying busy but my out-of-control emotions betrayed my grief. The children, ages five through twelve, experienced other forms of grief.

Trina, the oldest, needed to be the "braveheart." A facade of a strong, mature young adult came to the forefront, yet in private she wept and expressed her anger. It wasn't until years later that she confessed her hidden pain.

Jennifer chose seclusion, wrapping herself in her room like a caterpillar in a cocoon.

Years later, when I shared my pain regarding her words, "Mommy, God took the wrong parent," she cried, but she couldn't remember her words. I assured her that many children believe the deceased parent to be the perfect one. The remaining one is the "bad" parent until the grief diminishes.

A short time later, a beautiful letter flowed from her hand. In that letter, she assured me that the "right parent had lived." She needed me, not her father, in her life to enable her to mature and grow into the person God intended her to be.

Trevin, more than all the other children, manifested his anger and frustration outwardly. Not only grieved by his father's death, he feared losing me. Because I needed to be the main bread winner, I relinquished many of my motherly responsibilities to my twelve-year-old daughter. No matter how hard Trina tried to be the best "mother" she could, Trevin's young seven-year-old mind fought her attempts at motherhood. His heart and mind would not allow anyone else to take my place.

Jeremy, the youngest, remained the most untouched. He cried occasionally but consolation came easily. Both older sisters smothered him with love and affection, which he seemed to enjoy thoroughly. His memory of his father, to this day, remains vague.

As we each journeyed through our grief, we learned that we all suffer in unique ways. But God strengthened us and we learned to forgive each other for the mistakes we made because of misinterpreting those unique responses. Today, the close ties we share is a tribute to God's faithfulness.

My children most often asked me, "Why didn't you tell us more about what was happening?" and "Why couldn't we say good-bye to Daddy at the hospital?"

Because of their young ages, I not only had wanted to protect them but also needed to believe all would be well. My inadequate knowledge of a child's need for closure prevented me from taking them to the hospital the night he died. I was also afraid that his appearance in death would have a negative impact on them. Leaving them at home created misunderstanding and angry feelings for several years.

Now I can only look back and say to myself, "Jan, you did the best you could. Leave your children and their past grief in the Lord's hands. Trust Him to use the experience for their good and His glory."

—Jan Brunette

On The Winning Side Of Cancer

I was resting quietly in the recovery room when my surgeon silently appeared at my bedside. Without any preface, he gave the biopsy report: "It was cancer."

I felt numb; then the chilling shock began to whirl in my mind. He's talking breast cancer! I stared into his eyes; but it was hard to concentrate.

He went on. "You have a lot ahead of you. You will be facing surgery, pain and possibly weeks of radiation therapy. I think you can keep your breast, but I don't want you to think you'll get off easy. We will remove a number of lymph nodes under your arm—and there's pain with that."

After the surgeon gave me more information about the radiation oncologist I should see, he slipped out of the room. Tears stung my eyes, and I began to tremble. Then the words of Isaiah 41:10 came clearly to my mind: *Fear not, for I am with you, be not dismayed, for I am your God; I will strengthen you, I will help you, I will uphold you with my victorious right hand* (RSV).

Although I tasted salty tears in the corner of my quivering mouth, I sensed God's tender presence. He *was* holding me.

Once released from the recovery room, I was helped into our car. My husband, Bob, sat quietly behind the wheel, his face ashen. I didn't know what to say. I felt a tremendous love for him and we hugged. He told me that the surgeon had talked to him before me, and had asked, "How will she take it?" Bob had replied, "She'll be very optimistic."

My journey began in March, 1987. I was one of those healthy women in her late 40's who had never been concerned about the dreaded disease, breast cancer. I was a committed third-grade teacher, a free-lance writer, and most of all, the wife and mother in a wonderful family.

On April 6, 1987, I went into the hospital for a lumpectomy (removal of the tumor and surrounding tissue). I also had surgical preparations for a radiation implant in my breast. A number of lymph nodes were removed from under my arm to help the surgeon determine how far the cancer had spread.

The morning after surgery, my radiation oncologist risked his own health in a long-term way when he placed a radiation implant in my treated breast with his bare hands. The implant consisted of high-intensity radioactive pellets or seeds set in tiny plastic catheters. It was very moving to think of what he was doing to get me well!

I was kept in isolation in a private hospital room while the implant was in my body. Family and friends could make brief visits, although they had to sit behind a portable shield stationed across the room. Bob, in his usual humor, brought a sign and hung it over my bed: "Radioactive Woman Aboard."

Several days later the oncologist removed all of the materials and the radioactive seeds—again with bare hands. During the post-operative pain and isolation, I had many opportunities to focus on my Lord. I was in a constant attitude of prayer and I was able to read short portions of the Bible. Continually, I sensed the Lord saying to me, "Keep looking intently to Me!" This became my spiritual strategy for combating fear. My spiritual eyes seemed to be steadily noticing how God was working as my healer.

One day the surgeon told me reassuring news. The cancer had not spread to the lymph nodes under my arm!

A few weeks later I began five weeks of daily trips to the hospital for radiation treatments. I decided I would always think of a Scripture or hymn while I held still for each x-ray treatment. But when the buzzer droned for my first treatment, I was so stunned I couldn't think of a verse! Instead, as I held perfectly still, I prayed, *In the name of the Father, the Son and the Holy Spirit.* I took the powerful radiation treatments as almost a sacrament.

Throughout this experience, countless people prayed for me and did all sorts of thoughtful things. I saw it all as God's love in action. My husband demonstrated endless love and encouragement. Our college daughter, Karen, and our teenage son, John, also reached out to me in touching ways. And my third grade students overpowered me with notes, cards, and even a pasted collage about my life.

My recovery went well, but sometimes slowly. As my surgeon had said, it wasn't easy. There was pain, and for a long time, lingering fatigue. But I consistently experienced God's wondrous blessings, even as I dealt with the shock, fear and sometimes denial of my disease.

It's been ten years now since I had cancer. At each checkup, the doctors affirm that I am well. I give the praise to God through Christ, and I still hear His call, "To keep looking intently to Me."

—Charlotte Adelsperger

The Value Of A Penny

It seemed odd that the day of Lisa's passing came and went so . . . softly. I rather expected it to be more traumatic. Perhaps it was because we had known the end was coming for such a long time, that when it finally did come, it was just a "letting go."

How odd to feel no fear of death, only a quiet sadness. Even that softened and blew away as the days went by. Seeing the incredible peace that transformed her countenance in death seemed to help me focus on where she had gone, and that she was well. I thought of her waking in heaven, surprised at what she had never known she couldn't do . . . able then to do so much more. In her handicapped earthly body, she hadn't walked or talked, but in heaven she not only did that, but was laughing, singing and praising God. I had always believed anyone who knows Jesus experiences an undercurrent of joy and I discovered it was true . . . even in the sadness of loss.

Jesus made all the difference for me, but not for my eighteen-year-old niece, Penny. Even with all the years of Sunday school, Penny didn't really know Jesus. But she had loved her cousin Lisa devotedly, caring for her whenever the families were together, which was often. It appeared that Penny took the news of Lisa's passing well enough; but inside, the fear of death haunted her.

God seeks those He loves, and He was seeking Penny—He sought her even in her dreams. Not long before Lisa passed on, Penny dreamed that Lisa was talking with Jesus as they walked alongside a stream in Yosemite.

The Lord said, "I'm going to take you home soon."

"Please, not yet," Lisa implored, "I haven't told my family I love them."

"Don't worry," He said, "They know."

The Lord was preparing Penny.

The day before Lisa's memorial service, Penny came with the

family to the mortuary, but she waited outside the viewing room, refusing to see her cousin.

Her mother paused as she came out and said, "You really should go in. She looks so different."

Penny's curiosity got the best of her, and going in, she saw for herself the transformation that peace had made for Lisa. The Lord was gently loosing the grip of Penny's fear.

Not long after, Penny had another dream about Lisa. This time she saw her as she arrived in heaven. She was on the sidewalk in front of their great-grandparent's house. It sat on a hill with a flight of steps leading from the sidewalk up to a small yard in front. The front wall of the house was missing, like a doll house opened for play.

As Lisa stepped onto the sidewalk, she was no longer the retarded, handicapped infant in a 15-year-old body. She was a radiantly-healthy teen who took in her surroundings with intelligent eagerness. She wore a long, red-checked dress, trimmed in white lace, with a white apron.

A boy her same age, wearing a black tuxedo and a big smile, met her and said, "Hello, Lisa. We've been waiting for you. I'm supposed to accompany you up to your grandparents." He offered her his left arm and escorted her up the stairs with light, happy steps.

At the top, the young man gallantly walked her to the front door and cheerily told her he would see her later. Grandma welcomed her with a quaint gesture, then wrapped her in a warm embrace.

"We've been looking forward to your arrival! Come on inside," Grandma said.

Grandpa sat at her feet making root beer on the front porch. At his side was the familiar little poodle that Penny remembered so well. A wonderful smile for Lisa lit his face as he rose to greet her. She was home, whole and happy, with people who knew and loved her. Then she meet the others who had gone before her. Soon she'd meet Jesus.

When Penny told us her dream, those of us in the family who

were older saw elements in her dream that Penny couldn't have known. As she described the young man in the tux, we realized it was Ricky, a cousin who passed on years earlier, soon after letting his pastor know he had accepted Jesus. He had been the ringbearer in the wedding of Penny's parents, wearing a tux like she described. Also, like Lisa, he had been born with a severe problem, a heart defect. Just like us, Ricky's parents were told their child would die very young, but he too had his life extended to age fifteen. The gesture Penny saw Grandma use was one we recognized, but she had never seen, nor did she know Grandpa had ever made root beer. The dress she saw Lisa wearing was the one Lisa wore about the same age Ricky had been when he wore the tux.

God is still at work in Penny, though not often through dreams. She has no memory now of the fear of death that once haunted her. Jesus' love replaced it. No life is insignificant to Him; He values every Penny.

—Teresa Daniels

God's Protection

My three-year-old son was staying with his father for the weekend and I had a few friends over that evening. When they left around midnight, I noticed a neighbor man with running-weights on his legs hanging around the sidewalk in front of my house. Thinking that was strange, I dead-bolted my front and back doors.

At 4 a.m., I awoke to a noise in the house. I had been sleeping with my back facing the bedroom door and sensed someone standing nearby. In a panic, I prayed, "Please, Lord save me . . . don't let me die. I have a young son who needs me."

I heard the intruder walk closer and stand over me. My heart was thumping so loud, I knew he could hear it. In my fear, I imagined he would kill me so I decided to see who my killer was. I turned over in bed and saw that it was the same man who had stood in the yard when my friends had left.

I could not believe what came out of my mouth next, because the words did not reflect how I felt. I said in a light and genuinely curious tone, "Hi! What are you doing here?"

I must have surprised him because he stuttered at first and then responded, "Oh, I saw that your back door was open and I thought I would check to make sure you were OK"

I was trying to think but my body started to shake. I had pulled the covers up around my neck because I didn't have anything on. He saw my nervousness, moved on top of me outside the covers, and began kissing me. I started to cry but heard myself say, "Will you do me a favor and go check my son's bedroom . . . I want to make sure no one is in the house."

To my amazement, he got off me and walked down the very short hallway to my son's bedroom. I quickly got up, flung my robe around me and met him in the hallway as he returned. From that moment, I knew God had control. I started talking fast, saying things like, "What would I have done if you hadn't noticed someone trying to get into my house? It's so good to have a caring neighbor like you." He listened and agreed.

"Will you help me check the windows to make sure they're locked?" I inquired, aggressively leading the way from window to window. After all the windows were checked, I asked him to sit down on the living room couch and requested his name. "Mark," he replied. I told him my son occasionally played with his son.

Mark began complaining about his horrible home life and the difficulties with his wife. I listened intently, trying to give him sound advice. Wanting to be as unattractive as I could, I repeatedly sniffed, picked my nose, and scratched my head.

I looked up at the clock and it was 5 a.m. I spoke up, "I'm so tired, I better get some sleep." I walked over to the front door and held it open for him to leave. He walked out the door and I immediately dead-bolted the door and secured the chain. He knocked on the door within seconds. "What do you want?" I called out.

"Can you please not tell anybody about this?"

I replied, "No problem, I won't say a word."

At that moment, it felt like God released me from His grip, and I started to tremble uncontrollably. I remembered the Lord's promise, "I will never leave you nor forsake you," and I wept.

Six months later, Mark and his family moved out of the neighborhood.

Six years after that, I was producing a job fair when I looked across the room and recognized a particular man but couldn't remember how. I started walking toward him when it hit me. It was Mark, but it was too late to retreat. I walked up to him and inquired, "How are you? Do you remember me?" When he didn't answer, I continued, "Are you here looking for a job? Where do you live now?"

It was obvious he was very nervous and avoided most of my questions. I walked away three minutes later with more confidence than I could have ever anticipated. He was scared of me! Oh, thank you, Lord for that healing moment. I'm no longer afraid of him. I realized that my confidence and trust in the Lord had grown through that terrible experience so many years earlier. God had used it for good!

—Janet McCracken

Homesick For Heaven

The older I get and the longer I live, it seems that I have more friends and relatives in heaven than on earth! Even on a recent vacation to my home town, I visited more cemeteries than homes and decorated graves of the dead instead of taking gifts to the living. Heaven is becoming more precious all the time and earth holds less enchantment for me.

When my mother became terminally ill, she began to designate which relative was to inherit each of her belongings. Toward the end, each visitor was given a keepsake to take with them that very day. She was gradually divesting herself of the possessions accumulated during her long life.

Just this last Christmas, I decided to give away some of my own keepsakes that my granddaughters had casually mentioned wanting upon my death. But they quickly reassured me that they hoped I would live even longer than my mother, who died at 83, and my grandmother, who died at 95.

Sue, my oldest granddaughter at 27, wanted a new Bible for Christmas but wasn't sure what version or size. She lives in another state and couldn't get home for Christmas. This gave me the opportunity to give her one of my old Bibles. Earlier she had commented, "Your old Bibles are real heirlooms, Granny, with all the underlined passages and notes in the margin!"

Inside the old Bible, I put a check and a note telling Sue to use it to buy herself a new Bible. I told her that I hoped her new one would be as much a blessing to her as my old one had been to me over the years. I also stressed that though my old Bible had pages that were tattered and coming loose from the binding, "Bibles that are coming apart belong to people who aren't."

For Melanie, another granddaughter in her mid-twenties, who has her own apartment and entertains frequently, I wrapped up the set of bone china that I had inherited from a relative who brought it from her childhood home in England. Melanie had long admired it. Her sister, Sue, will eventually get the blue crystal set I still use, just as Melanie will later get another of my worn-out Bibles and a check for a new one.

As time goes by, I will probably give away even more of my material possessions while I am alive, instead of waiting until death draws close.

The older I get, the more I want to see my Savior. Each year I grow more homesick for heaven. Not only will I be reunited there with my loved ones who have gone on before, but I will meet my Savior face to face!

—Delores Elaine Bius

Miracle In El Salvador

"Oh, Eli, what could have happened?" I tried not to whine. "Ernest still isn't home."

"I can't understand it," my husband frowned. "John said the team would come back early today." The concern in Eli's voice increased my fears. Life in El Salvador had become scary. I depended on Eli's reassurance. Now he was alarmed and I didn't like it.

Things had seemed peaceful enough that morning. Thirteen-year-old Ernest, grinning broadly, had waved at us as the red pickup roared away. I felt better then about letting him go. The decision hadn't been easy. I hardly let my children out of my sight. But Ernest wanted to be free.

"May I go to the coast with the relief team?" he begged. "I'd like to see the flood damage."

Reports of recent killings flashed through my mind. A girl had been shot in her car for not stopping at a checkpoint. On a school trip, Ernest had seen a pile of corpses beside the road. I didn't want him exposed to violence, but what could I do?

"Ernest," I finally said, "I think there will be enough volunteers without you."

"But, Mother," he wailed, "John said there's room for me. I could count pills for the nurse or hand out soap—anything. Please let me go."

My need to protect Ernest conflicted with his need to grow up, so Eli and I finally consented. *There won't be much danger*, we reasoned. *Ernest will be back by early afternoon.*

Something had gone wrong. Afternoon faded into evening. The team still hadn't returned.

"Eli," I began again, "Isn't there someone we can call?"

He shook his head. "The telephone lines are out because of the flood. There's nothing we can do but pray. We'll just have to trust God."

Trust God! But what if they'd been captured by guerrillas? Or worse, what if John had driven through a checkpoint? Soldiers often patrolled the mountain the group would cross. John was new in El Salvador. Why hadn't we warned him?

Trust God! I wanted to trust God. I pretended that I did, but fear still haunted me.

I know God *could* protect us, but I wasn't sure if He *would*. Other missionaries had trusted God and some of them had been killed. Still, my husband believed. Why couldn't I?

"Lord," I pleaded, "Please protect Ernest. Help me trust You."

At ten o'clock that night, headlights turned into our driveway. We heard a scramble as the relief team jumped off the truck.

"Thank God, we're alive!" they exclaimed in shaking voices. "We drove through a checkpoint. John didn't see the soldiers in time. They shot at us."

"Ernest?" I gasped. "Where's Ernest?"

"He was hit by bullet fragments but they were removed in the hospital. Here he comes now."

Ernest, pale and shaken, limped to the couch. I slumped beside him, stroking his soft, blond hair. I couldn't get enough of seeing him and feeling his warm, living body.

"All the soldiers were near my window," said Ernest. "When I heard the shots and saw fire flying from their rifles, I curled up under the dash. Suddenly, I felt a sharp pain. The seat of my pants was sticky with blood."

I trembled as the group described their narrow escape. "Those of us on the back of the truck lay flat on the floor. Bullets whistled over our heads and ripped into the metal all around us. Finally the shooting stopped. Dozens of soldiers stepped out of the darkness and surrounded us. They aimed their rifles at us, their fingers on the triggers. They yelled, 'Hands up! Lie down on the road!'

"The commander asked where we'd come from. We told him we'd taken relief to the flood victims. When he realized we weren't guerrillas, he asked if anyone was hurt."

"I told him I was," said Ernest. "He ordered me to my feet but I fainted when I got up."

The team nurse spoke up, "The soldiers rushed Ernest to the hospital in an army truck."

"On the way," Ernest said, "I heard the soldiers asking who started the shooting. They seemed sorry about their mistake."

Eli and I stepped outside to see the bullet-riddled truck. I almost fainted when I saw bullet holes dotted all over. The window on Ernest's side was gone. All the remaining windows were perforated. Bullet holes punctured the ceiling, floor, seat, and dash. A battalion of soldiers had shot at ten persons at close range without killing anyone. It was a miracle!

But a greater miracle took place in me.

That night, assurance began to replace my fear. it's not that I think God will necessarily keep me from harm and death. He may not always shield me from the dreadful things I used to fear. But now I trust him to help me face whatever He allows me to experience.

I'm learning that even in El Salvador, God can be trusted.

—Verda J. Glick

Giving Thanks In All Things

As the mother of eleven children, all nearly grown and doing well, my friend Marge was particularly blessed. But then tragedy struck her family: her daughter-in-law died in childbirth. Marge desired that her response be right.

"Please, Lord," she prayed. "You must give me something to be thankful for."

Marge came up with a list of eight praises, some of them little things that might not mean much to another person; but they helped her perspective.

Only months later, her daughter Dana was killed in an automobile accident. Again my friend sought the Lord for specific things that she could be thankful for, like Dana didn't suffer long and the children weren't in the car. Her reasons for praise on Dana's list reached seventeen.

Marge explained, "I'm not thankful that my daughter died, but God gives us things to be thankful for in our calamities. These thanksgiving lists were the very things that helped me not to sink under the river of grief. They kept my head above water. Even though I was going through a rough time, I could still see God working."

My friend is a beautiful testimony of God's sustaining grace in great difficulty. In the midst of heartache, she's been given the gift of a thankful heart.

—Cynthia Culp Allen

The Value Of Suffering

Grief and mourning are a necessary part of growing through the hard times. Through your suffering God will help you to recover and will give you something positive out of it all. You who have endured the stinging experiences are the choicest counselors God can use! Remember, I've been there, too. In the midst of your grief, just hang on to the idea that this too will pass, and God will use it for good.

Here's an illustration to help you see the value in suffering. A bar of iron worth $2.50, when wrought into a horseshoe, is worth $5.00; if made into needles it is worth $175.00; if into penknife blades, it is worth $1,625. If it's made into springs for watches, it is worth $125,000. What a "trial by fire" that bar must undergo to be worth this! But the more it is manipulated, and the more it is hammered and passed through the heat, beaten, pounded, and polished, the greater its value.

—Barbara Johnson

10

Material Loss

*I know what it is to be in need, and I know what it is to
have plenty. I have learned the secret of being content
in any and every situation, whether well fed or
hungry, whether living in plenty or in want.*

Philippians 4:12

A Friend's Offer

The recession brought the pressure of negative cash flow. Can you think of any feeling more gloomy than financial pressure? Robert and I had been friends for a dozen years. We just clicked. Our mutual interest in business was a factor, but our personalities also meshed.

So it was natural for me to visit with Robert when my business problems were bigger than my own ingenuity. He listened patiently for a couple of hours. It was good for me to be able to sort out my thinking.

Then Robert said a remarkable thing. Maybe I thought he would give advice that would magically turn around the business. Perhaps I had been looking for some encouragement. But what he said floored me.

"I don't have any answers, but if the worst comes to pass," he said, "I've got enough money for the both of us to live on. Whatever I have is yours."

There was something about the way he said it, Robert wasn't just joking around. He really meant what he said. Of course, I could never take up Robert's offer, but his act of true friendship reminded me of the God who owns the cattle on a thousand hills.

Suddenly, the problems seemed minuscule. I knew God would provide for me. By being my friend, Robert had shown me how much God loved me, and I knew I would be all right.

—Patrick M. Morley

Run With Endurance

Disaster struck my family early January 1, 1960. As 1959 earned its exit, the last guests bid farewell to my parents after their New Year's Eve celebration. Mom, who preferred to have a clean house before retiring for the night, pushed herself to finish the task while Dad fell into bed. Finally, washing the last dish at 3 a.m., she slipped into bed. The house was tidy, us six kids were sound asleep, and my aunt was comfortable on the couch having her last cigarette.

Mom and Dad, who had little in the way of wealth, worked hard to make Christmas special. Our beautiful Christmas tree stood in the corner of the living room with a few of our newly-opened presents scattered underneath.

Just as Mom slipped into a deep sleep, she suddenly awakened for some unknown reason. She quickly sat up, realizing there was a strong smell of smoke filtering into their bedroom! She immediately shook my Dad, who stirred but remained asleep. With one last forceful jar, she screamed at him to wake up, then she frantically raced to the bedroom door. The thick smoke was rapidly filling the house and raging flames devoured anything that dared to resist its command.

Compelled by a mother's love, she was determined to save us from the deadly fire. Holding her breath, she crawled along the wall to our bedroom that housed all six kids. But the big wooden bed that held us three younger kids stood directly in front of the window—the only means of escape! Attempting any other route would surely mean death. With mere seconds to act, Mom miraculously began to break apart the heavy antique headboard!

Feeling my dad's heavy breathing behind her, she motioned him to climb out the window. The toxic smoke was tormenting his one-lung condition. One by one, we were briskly tossed into my dad's waiting arms.

Several fire engines with bright red lights twirling and loud sirens blaring, clamored towards us as we fled for our lives. Once outside and clinging to each other, we turned around to witness the all-powerful flames shooting through the windows. My aunt joined us staring at the merciless blaze as it completely erased our dreams. We stood motionless, in our pajamas. No shoes. No coats. Only covered by a blanket of snow.

Several of the firemen, accepting that it was useless to fight this one, took off their coats to wrap around our shoulders, and placed us in the front seat of the fire engine. An older fireman, who had tears in his eyes, approached my mom and dad, gently placing his coat on their shoulders.

When it finally ended, the only item recovered was an old bottle full of loose change. This senseless tragedy had been caused by my aunt who fell asleep with a lit cigarette.

"It was purely a miracle anyone survived," said one of the firemen.

"That mother really has some kind of love for her family," said another.

And still, another remarked, "There must have been angels helping to tear that bed apart!"

When reality finally set in, we realized we had less than nothing. There was no insurance for anything, including the newly-acquired presents.

My dad, a proud man, knew this was beyond even his fortitude. He humbly called the Red Cross for assistance. To his disillusionment, they refused. Their question was, "Are you working?" His answer, of course, was "yes."

"At least we have our lives, honey," my mom said. "We could never replace those."

The bottle of loose change, totaling $78.23, would be used for new shoes. We must have been a curious sight when the six of us marched out of the shoe store on that unforgettable day. The sparkle in our eyes mirrored the elation in our hearts.

Together, my parents began the arduous climb out of their overwhelming dilemma, never giving up on each other and not buckling under the severe weight of life's pressures.

As sure as the rains come here in Washington state, my parents were and are dependable. With Dad's stubbornness and Mom's determination, they unequivocally moved forward without looking back. Their marriage has been full of an assortment of highs and lows, building and rebuilding, and most of all, love.

Not even the doctor's diagnosis that Dad would only live to be 30 from his lung condition could deter them. He just turned 65 and retired two years ago from a career as a hard-working carpenter. Mom's rheumatoid arthritis may have crippled her hands and feet, but not her will. Through all of life, they have remained hand-in-hand, prepared to cross the finish line, for better or worse.

—Janie Ness

208 **GOD'S VITAMIN "C" FOR THE HURTING SPIRIT**

Shelter In The Storm

On my knees, I cried, "Lord, please stop the storm, I want it to be over." I remembered parts of Jonah's prayer, *You hurled me into the deep, into the very heart of the seas, and the currents, swirled about me, all your waves and breakers swept over me* (Jonah 2:3). My storm had lasted two years and today I felt windswept, water logged, and ready to drown.

Two years ago my husband Bob lost his job and with it many of his friends and most of his dreams. He's spent the past year training for the position of locomotive engineer. As a trainee, he has no schedule, long hours and little pay. Just last week the company informed him there are no positions available and he will remain a trainee indefinitely. As I look at the mounting bills with no end in sight, I'm ready for the waves to wash me overboard!

"Please, God, let this storm pass!" I prayed over and over throughout that day.

The next day dawned a beautiful March morning. It did not match my mood. I got the kids off to school and sat down for my morning devotional. I was discouraged and ready to pray again, "Let the storm end!"

Thinking I should pray for shelter and peace in the midst of the storm, I began my devotional, but it wasn't long until I was over-whelmed with despair and prayed instead, "God, I want it to end!"

Then I remembered another storm that occurred about twenty years earlier. I had come home from college on the weekend and, since it was a beautiful 72 degree day, I'd requested the use of Dad's canoe.

My father shuttled me, my brother, Tim, and Bob, my then fiancé, up the river for a leisurely canoe ride back home. About thirty minutes into our journey, we passed the last civilization we'd see for some hours to come. Suddenly, ahead between two mountain peaks, we saw a huge wall of black clouds. It was moving straight up the valley toward us.

As fast as they could, Tim and Bob paddled to a nearby island. But the storm hit us too fast. Rain pelted us, wind whipped the once calm water into large waves, and thunder echoed up and down the valley.

On the island we found shelter in a three-sided lean-to built from worn lumber. The much appreciated shack was probably built by an exploring band of boys.

We managed to start a fire with bits and pieces of our shelter. The storm raged around us and brought with it a 38 degree temperature drop. Though we didn't know it at the time, there were numerous tornadoes touching down all around us. Huddling close together, we waited out the three-hour deluge in relative comfort.

As the storm reduced itself to a drizzle, we prepared for our return journey down river. We were three hours behind schedule and concerned about my father who must be anxiously waiting. We would be fortunate to complete the trip before nightfall.

Bob and Tim paddled like men possessed. The temperature hung around 34 degrees and dressed only in shorts and T-shirts, we were thoroughly chilled. I felt like I was in a cramped, frigid prison. I shivered incessantly. I've never before or after been so cold and I hope to never be that cold again.

Remembering that storm as I enjoyed this beautiful Spring morning, I thought of that island shelter and the warmth provided by the fire as the wind and rain pummeled the earth all around us. We were comfortable and safe during the storm, but as we paddled home I was never so uncomfortable in all my life.

I became convinced to ask only for shelter in my financial storm and not necessarily the cessation of it. God will provide peace and comfort as the winds blow and the rains fall around us. Provision of the shelter in the midst of the storm is one of our Lord's demonstrations of His great compassion and mercy. He can be our shelter in the storm.

—T.A. Huggins

Waiting

I have always disliked waiting. My father drummed into his three children that we were late if we weren't five minutes early. Both my heritage and my impatient nature abhor waiting. Thus, when God puts me on hold, I begin to squirm. When He keeps me there, I fume, struggle, and strain. His patience with my impatience is incredible.

I am not talking about the times God says to wait while He works out a perfect way to say yes. Nor am I speaking of short-term delays. These are only wisps of fog swirling about the planes in the airport of our minds. But the dense fog of stripping is when all avenues of continuing are canceled with no promise of future flights.

The first time God's fog drifted into our lives was a year after Jack graduated from seminary. We'd been enjoying that year, a year of firsts for us: first full-time job in Christian ministry after seminary, first child (we didn't know then that she was to be our only one), first year I hadn't worked outside our home. Then, because of certain circumstances, God led Jack to resign his position as youth director. Another job opened immediately, but God wouldn't let us accept it.

It was then that the fog settled in—in earnest. For four months the three of us lived, first with my folks, and then with Jack's. Jack did everything from taking a government census of fruit trees to being a song leader for local evangelistic meetings. But no permanent job opened.

Each day I agonized and pleaded with God: "Please, Lord, open up the right job for us."

After two months of my begging, God began to deal with my heart. If He had spoken aloud, it couldn't have been clearer.

"Carole," He said accusingly, "you are anxious."

"Well, Father, I've certainly got something to be anxious about," I countered.

Then He reminded me, gently but firmly, of Philippians 4:6, which burned itself into my mind, *Do not be anxious about anything, but in everything, by prayer and petition, with thanksgiving, present your requests to God. Do not be anxious . . . .*

I can still remember the tears of confession and my cry for help. I stopped praying for a job to open up and began to pray about the attitude of my anxious heart. In a miraculous way, God gave me peace during the next two months before He gave us the job of His choice.

Sometimes, in the fog of waiting, the lesson He will pound home to us is simply, *Do not be anxious.* Our own helplessness causes us to cry to Him to give us strength and trust not to be anxious when everything within us screams with concern and apprehension. Over and over He whispers, "Trust Me." It takes all our will, and great help from Him, to do just that.

What helps us when everything is obscured? When we seem to be marking time? When the fog closes in with vengeance?

It helps me to hang on to the knowledge that *even the fog is preparing me for Heaven.*

—**Carole Mayhall**

A Season Of Receiving

My parents taught me early in life about the joy of giving. In their own way they modeled Jesus' teaching, *It is more blessed to give than to receive* (Acts 20:35). As I watched them share their money with others, it seemed natural that I would do the same when I grew up and had income of my own.

Their example made my transition easy. Several years ago my husband and I established a special checking/savings account for this purpose. We called it "God's Account." We deposited ten percent of all money we received into this fund to be used for church tithes and offerings and as gifts to missionaries and groups doing God's work.

The idea worked for us and we hoped it was pleasing to God. We followed this plan without fail—until a few years ago—when suddenly with little warning, we hit bottom financially.

My husband lost his job and my freelancing opportunities dwindled to almost nothing. Regardless of how hard we tried to find work, nothing turned up.

We prayed. We asked others to pray. We drew on our savings account. We cashed in investments. We sold some property. Before long we were using the last bit of reserves we had. I panicked! Then I became angry. Hadn't we followed the Lord's leading? Hadn't we obeyed and shared and given freely and joyfully? I felt betrayed.

"Why this, Lord?" I asked. "What have we done wrong? We want to work and earn our way. And we want to give to others. Please provide jobs and income for us."

The Lord did not answer my prayer in the way I had hoped. But He did answer. He did not bring us work right away, but He did provide for us.

One Sunday, my husband found an envelope addressed to him in the deacons' mail slot at church. It contained an encouraging passage from Scripture, an anonymous note, and enough cash to tide us over for a couple of weeks. About the time that ran out, people in our Bible study delivered unexpected gift checks one morning.

But the more people reached out to us, the more upset I became. This wasn't the way it was supposed to be. On the one hand, we needed their support, and on the other hand I felt uneasy as the obligations mounted. I was determined to get out of this position as fast as we could.

My part-time teaching helped keep us going awhile longer. but our bills were greater than my income, and we began to slip again. Then one month, when our rent was due and our checking account empty, my husband appealed to the Deacons' Fund at our church. The very group he headed!

To me that was the final blow. The Deacons' Fund! How humiliating! That was for people who couldn't make it. People who didn't have skills. People who were poor. People in real need. We had always *given* to the Fund. I never expected to *receive* from it.

When the check arrived from the Fund, I was caught between relief and resentment. I felt absolutely helpless. Then suddenly I realized how unaccustomed I was to receiving. It simply wasn't part of my lifestyle. And more to the point, I was downright uncomfortable with it. Receiving made me vulnerable to others and to the Lord. I had no control. People knew my needs. I didn't like it. It didn't fit my image of myself—the great giver!

But there was more to come. God wasn't finished with me yet. The following month we received a check from my parents who had not known the extent of our problems and for my husband's birthday, two or three gift checks appeared.

Then one afternoon, just before Christmas, we received a money order for the exact amount we needed for our tree, holiday food, and a few gifts. It was signed, "Barnabas." A fitting pseudonym! We looked at each other in disbelief. Then came the tears. "Praise God!" we shouted. For an entire year, despite our clumsy attempts to interrupt the process, He had kept us going.

It was all coming clear at last. It had been our season to receive, our time to be humbled before Him, our turn to acknowledge our weakness and our neediness before our brothers and sisters.

Then shortly after Christmas things began to turn around; almost as suddenly as they had fallen apart the year before. My freelance work picked up, and my husband received several promising job leads. Our hearts were full.

As I looked ahead with hope, I also looked back on our season of receiving with thanksgiving. The lesson I had learned from my parents so long ago was just as true in the present as it had been in the past. It simply took hold in a new and deeper way.

It *is* more blessed to give than to receive. But giving has more than one dimension, as the Lord had shown us. Real giving requires a humbled heart and a receptive spirit—one that also allows others to be blessed by the joy of giving.

—Karen O'Connor

Fireproof

The worst phone call I ever made was to my husband the day our house burned. Still cold and shaking from running door-to-door for help in sub-zero weather, I called Dan from a neighbor's house to tell him the bad news. He rushed home, not prepared for what he would encounter.

When he arrived, thick, black smoke was billowing from every window. Firefighters were smashing glass to release the heat before running into the house with hoses snaking behind them, ready to douse the blaze. Within minutes the flames were out. But our "trial by fire" was just beginning.

Dan stepped inside to assess the damage. Downstairs where the fire had started, he sloshed through a smoldering mess of week-old Christmas toys, a television that had melted to the floor and countless other unrecognizable items that had been destroyed by flames, intense heat and smoke. Our family room was a charred skeleton of beams and melted linoleum. Upstairs, black soot coated everything. Christmas ornaments dangled precariously from the brittle branches of our once-festive tree.

In a daze, Dan made his way toward the bedrooms. The noxious smell of melted plastic burned his nostrils. Halfway down the hall, a photograph lay on the floor. It was a treasured picture of Dan and me with the kids, ruined by smoke and water. Tears welled up in his eyes as he lifted the picture off the floor.

He had gone to work that day like any other, fully expecting to return to the comfort of home that evening. Instead, he came home to complete loss. Well, not complete loss. The things that mattered most to him—the children and me—were still safe and waiting for him across the street.

When Dan greeted us at our neighbor's house, I was afraid he might be angry about the fire. Neither one of us knew how it had started, but I felt responsible—I was the one home when it happened. My fears were unfounded. Dan embraced me with tenderness, concern and gratitude, thankful the only injuries were my sprained ankle and frostbite on our oldest son's toes.

As the day wore on, my shock dissipated—giving way to vivid images of smoke and panic and chaos. What would we do next? We had just moved into this house five months earlier, and being new to the city, we didn't have family or close friends to turn to. Recognizing my despair, Dan described his walk through our house, which now seemed more like a cave. He told me it was then that he realized the fire revealed something significant about us: In losing all of our possessions, we could see more clearly what we really have—each other and a home that cannot be destroyed by fire.

We spent the next two weeks in hotels. That first night, Dan and I lay entwined in our bed, while our three children slept soundly in the queen-size bed next to ours. The sound of their breathing was the sweetest lullaby I've ever heard. As Dan cradled me, a salty mixture of grief and joy began to wet my pillow.

Here we were without a house, yet I felt completely rooted and sheltered by his love. It was at that moment that I discovered what it means to have a sense of place. Mine is with Dan.

As I drifted off to sleep, the lyrics to the old Billy Joel song, *You're My Home*, ran through my mind. This had been our song years ago. What prophetic irony. With Dan by my side, I truly had "a roof above and good walls all around." Gradually, I dozed off with the song on my mind, Dan in my arms and a thankfulness to God that "wherever we're together, that's my home."

—**Marian V. Liautaud**

11

Heaven—Our Future Home

*Now we know that if the earthly tent we live in is
destroyed, we have a building from God, an eternal
house in the heaven, not built by human hands.*

II Corinthians 5:1

Reunion

From a side street a lawnmower whines,
In a towering Juniper
a wren tunes his instrument,
Two plots over a grasshopper munches
a dandelion—
Abrupt reminders that life goes on
as an unresponsive stone coldly
confirms your death—indifferent
in the absence of hugs, walks,
winks, and shared pain.

Pink carnations fail
to convey or console my loss.
The beflowered cross shading
the headstone can't obscure
my suffering. Longing
for the Reunion, I mourn
in the shadow of Your
hopeful Cross.

—**Mona Gansberg Hodgson**

The Shadow Of Death

A friend who had lost her brother to cancer when he was a teenager talked to our ladies' Bible study about the topic of death. Someone asked her how she had come through the ordeal without being angry at God.

"At first I didn't want to think that God would allow such a terrible thing to happen to people who loved Him," she said. "I was angry and felt very alone.

"Then I ran across the verse in the 23rd Psalm that talks *about the valley of the shadow of death*. I realized that, in order for something to have a shadow, it had to have light behind it. God's presence was the light behind my brother's death. We knew that in the end Daniel was going to be in the presence of that Light, and that gave us comfort."

In his book, *God's Psychiatry* (Revelation), Charles Allen talks about a real Valley of the Shadow of Death. It is located in Palestine and leads from Jerusalem to the Dead Sea. Surrounded by an ominous mountain range, the narrow and dangerous pathway is rough and the possibility of death ever present. It is a forbidding journey that one dreads to take. But the sheep are not afraid. Why? Because the shepherd is alongside.

—Kayleen J. Reusser

A Message From Home

Oh dear family, please do not mourn too long for me,
We are all just passing through this life you see.
This place was meant to be a temporary home,
I went back to heaven to worship by His golden throne.
When we go, our spirits are gathered to our loved ones,
Just remember, we are all with the Lord's Son.
We live in the mansion, past the moon, to the right,
Up the hill, close by, our Lord's precious sight.
Please ask the Lord Jesus to come into your hearts,
So we can remain together, so we will never part.
Please, don't be dismayed about my passing over,
I'm singing and rejoicing and dancing in clover.

—Deborah Kaye Adamo

The Road Alone

Not long ago I used to think that
   being alone was to be dreaded;
   traveling an unmapped, winding road
   unable to see where you're headed;
   zigzagging and flip-flopping until
   all sense of direction is shredded.

But down the road, around a few curves,
   breath-taking vistas ensnare the eyes;
   disquiet fades in awareness of
   the Creator's presence to advise;
   a close and abiding companion
   whose cloud and fire emblazon the skies.

Now I realize the road alone
   isn't the highway to loneliness
   but a journey through faith's countryside
   with the Paraclete as a buttress
   while He leads me down an unmapped road
   in sync with the goals of our express.

*Whom have I in heaven but thee? and there is none upon earth that
I desire beside thee. My flesh and my heart faileth: but God is the
strength of my heart, and my portion forever* (Psalm 73:25, 26 KJV).

—**Dave Evans**

I'm Free

Don't grieve for me
   For now I'm free,
   I'm following the path
   God laid for me.
   I took his hand when
   I heard his call,
   I turned my back, and left it all.
   I could not stay another day
   to laugh, to love, to walk or play
   Tasks left undone must stay that way,
   I've found that peace at the close of the day.
   If my parting has left a void
   Then fill it with remembered joy,
   A friendship shared, a laugh, a kiss
   Ah, yes, these things I too will miss.
   Be not burdened with times of sorrow,
   I wish the sunshine of tomorrow.
   My life's been full, I savored much,
   Good friend, good times,
   A loved one's touch.
   Perhaps my time seemed all too brief,
   Don't lengthen it now with
   Undue grief.
   Lift up your heart and share with me
   God wanted me now
   He set me free!

—James Donovan, 18-years-old
Written in honor of his grandmother after her death.

12

Loss Of A Dream

"For I know the plans I have for you," declares the Lord, "plans to prosper you and not to harm you, plans to give you hope and a future."

Jeremiah 29:11

The Final Score Of Trouble

One of my all-time favorite sports memories is of the final hockey game played in the 1980 Winter Olympics in Lake Placid, New York. Facing Scandinavian and Eastern Block teams composed of seasoned veterans who had given their lives to the state to prepare for and compete in the Olympic matches, the American team, made up for the most part of amateur players from colleges and universities, seemed on paper to be no match. The Olympics came at a time when the spirit of Americans was at an all-time low. It seemed Americans had little to cheer about.

Yet the American team persisted and won game after game. I came home from church on the Sunday that our boys were playing the Russians. I turned on the television and noted, much to my surprise, that though the match was more than half over, we were playing head-to-head with the Russians. I sat down and could hardly move. I watched with anxiety as our men skated, and flinched every time the Russians cocked their sticks to make a shot. I relaxed in relief when I saw that they hadn't scored. It was an agonizing, white-knuckled, tight-stomached spectator event for me and many others who watched across the country. Then, in the final moments it became obvious that we might beat the Russians. It seemed impossible. It seemed so wonderful—at last we had something to cheer about. We had done it.

That night after church, the network decided to replay the hockey game. We invited some friends over to enjoy the game with us. I sat back in my easy chair with a glass of Pepsi® in my hand and a bowl of popcorn on my lap. I enjoyed every moment of the game. No whitened knuckles, no tight stomach. What made the difference?

What I knew.

What I knew to be true! The outcome was secure.

Though we don't know the final score in trouble, we do know that in God the outcome is secure. No matter what it is, it is unshakably scheduled for grace, growth, and glory.

—Joseph M. Stowell

Accepting The Empty Nest

Soon after our eldest son, Dick, left for college, I went in to tidy up his room. Perched on his baseball bat sat his dusty cap, just as he had always left it. Suddenly, I felt like that bat and cap were no longer needed by my son.

Dick had been a baseball pitcher, basketball player, and golfer in high school, and watching him play had been a major part of our family's social life. But now, he was far away at college, and I knew I wouldn't see him again for many months.

When our second child, Liz, left for college, I experienced a similar sense of abandonment. Luckily, her college was closer, so she could make weekend visits home.

Two years later, our youngest child, Doug, went away to school. Now the house took on a stark quietness. The phone hardly rang, and we lost contact with the friends we had seen at our children's school events.

In an effort to fill the void, I threw myself into two part-time jobs. Shortly after, my husband's father died and his 80-year-old mother moved in with us. Because she was unable to drive, I chauffeured her to all her appointments.

My schedule was busier than ever—too busy, I discovered. Driving home from work one day, I blacked out briefly while stopped at a traffic light. Fear gripped me when I regained consciousness. *Am I having a stroke?* I prayed for help to get home safely. When I arrived, I went straight to bed.

My doctor examined me a few days later. He found nothing seriously wrong, but told me I was suffering from a "burned-out condition." He advised me to quit at least one of my jobs.

At first, I resisted. Staying home would only remind me of how much I missed my children. But I was so tired that I forced myself to rest.

My husband suggested a vacation to California. There I took in the sunshine, read books, took long walks, and reflected. I realized that I had gone through a series of major changes—my children leaving, starting the part-time jobs, and having my mother-in-law move in. There had been little time to adjust.

Understanding this did not immediately solve my problems, however. After we returned home, I ate poorly, grabbing whatever was in sight for meals. I lost weight and found myself crying frequently. I could not drive, for fear I would black out again.

This time, the doctor diagnosed my condition as anxiety. Not sure what this meant, I went to a second doctor. He agreed I had anxiety, as well as possible change-of-life symptoms.

Both physicians prescribed mild tranquilizers. I was reluctant to take them, but I found that half a pill did calm me down and made my life more manageable.

I began to see that my health problems stemmed not only from the loss of my children and the other changes in my life, but from the loss of my identity. Being a mother was no longer my primary role. I needed to develop a new lifestyle.

To begin with, I needed to take better care of myself physically. With the help of my mother-in-law, I learned to eat meals regularly again and to slay on a balanced diet. I also began to exercise more.

Now that I wasn't working, I began walking our dog three times a day instead of once. At my husband's suggestion, I got out my dusty, old bicycle and started to ride again. I contacted a friend from church who has also had health problems and invited her to join me.

As a way to meet some of my spiritual needs, I joined a women's Bible class. I have found it helpful to share my feelings with other members of the group.

Inevitably, there have been setbacks. I experienced another loss when our new pastor decided to assume responsibility for the church newsletter, which I had edited. But I took a writing course and began to submit articles for publication. Writing has given me a new purpose and sense of being needed.

Lately, I have taken on a different challenge. My husband has been teaching me how to play golf. Walking on God's green earth has done wonders for me.

It has not been easy to let go of my children. However, I have learned through this experience that God does not abandon us. When a person or role we love is taken away, God can bring us to a new understanding of who we are and of who He is.

—Gloria H. Dvorak

Martha's Gift

After earning my RN, I married a medical student. We set out to save the world, but during his internship our first child was born and I left my short-lived career to become a full-time mother, a choice freely made. Occasionally when asked if I would re-enter nursing, I answered, "No." I was aware that medical advances had left me behind. I was involved with children and church endeavors and began to nurture a desire to write.

Time passed quickly. My nest was emptying, and with it much of my purpose in life. I prayed for direction. To my surprise, God seemed to be calling me back into nursing. My cap was dusty and my skills rusty, but if this was where God wanted me, I would try.

Re-entry was another story. I needed a refresher course, but we lived in rural California, and my calls to nearby hospitals were disappointing. Classes refused nurses over two years out of practice. How much could one forget in two years? How much in twenty?

"See, God?" I gloated, with relief. "I told you so!"

Then, in a newspaper I read that the University of California at Davis was offering a refresher course for nurses—regardless of years. Chagrined, I dialed the number.

On a sunny September morning I arrived at the Sacramento extension offices with eight other equally-nervous "mature" nurses, to be "refreshed." Two instructors, who had been huddled with a telephone, finally approached us. There were two drop-outs. Our group was too small, so the class was canceled.

Racing to my car, I smugly drove home, sure that God had finally seen his error and released me to other pursuits. He knew I wasn't up to re-entry.

As I sat in my kitchen sipping iced tea and contemplating my future, the phone jarred my tranquillity. Several nurses with financial needs had remained behind and persuaded the school to offer the class if each student would pay an additional sum to cover the drop-outs' tuition.

Would I agree? Can I deny these other women the class? Maybe I could pay and not attend? What are you doing to me, God? Contrite, I wrote my check.

Once in class, discouragement gnawed at me. Years of conversing with children had taken their toll on concentration. Despair followed.

Our first day of clinical practice would have been funny if it hadn't been so pathetic. We shuffled like kindergartners in the hospital lobby. On the nursing unit I felt clumsy and ill-at-ease. Young nurses were running around in gaily-colored smocks, unlike the whitewashed world I remembered. Having instructors around was enough to unnerve anyone. Everything felt wrong. Almost desperately now, I wanted out.

Then one fateful day I met Martha, who at twenty-nine had been pulled from icy waters and revived by CPR. Her brain-dead body was slumped in bed with her head rolled too high. She was soaked with perspiration, though the room felt cold. Martha reeked of urine, and gray-green froth oozed around the oxygen cup over the breathing tube in her throat. The ventilator rhythmically wheezed. I turned away, sick and angry.

Whose work is this? I fumed. *Who presumed to bring function back to this once-dead body? Someone pounded her heart and pumped her lungs and produced this—this non-person. Who was playing God?*

I was pulled from my funk by gurgling sounds. Martha was drowning again—in her own secretions.

My reluctant eyes drifted toward the suction apparatus and I gagged. I always gagged when performing tracheal suction. It was the one function in nursing that I had not been able to handle.

Martha sputtered again. I reached for the suction catheter and noted with surprise its familiar feel. Having cleared her airway, I began to clean the thickly-crusted tube, thankful that she was oblivious to my uncontrolled gagging. With Martha freely breathing, I rolled up my sleeves and went to work. Gut-level nursing remained unchanged.

When a relief nurse slipped into the room two hours later, Martha was clean and dry. She was bathed, fed and massaged. Her hair was brushed, her mouth fresh, and she lay propped on her side with plump pillows supporting her well-aligned body. Martha had been pampered and was sleeping deeply. She was at peace and so was I.

Martha was transferred to a hospital nearer her parents' home where she later quietly died. I spent the next several years practicing nursing in other places. Martha's family never knew me, but I never forgot their daughter. I entered her room unnerved, upset and filled with grave doubts. I left knowing that I had never really stopped being a nurse after all.

God's gift to me through Martha was the recognition that as long as I have the ability to serve, I must do all that I can, leaving my unanswered questions about quality of life with God, who is the only one who can know the full potential of any life. Martha gave me the assurance that I had a place in nursing and that a love of people had never left me.

—Marilyn J. Hathaway

Wounded Relationship

From the moment she knew she had conceived, she had loved her son. Now, as an adult, he had suddenly put up a wall between them. No more would he take her in his arms. No more would he come to her home. A wall was there, a wall so impenetrable that it could not be bulldozed down.

The pain was enormous. She could think of nothing else. He felt she had failed him as a mother. And she had. She hadn't meant to . . . but was it as bad as he thought it was? Was it an incurable failure? One that would cripple him and their relationship forever?

The pain was excruciating. All of her life her goal had been to be a good mother and wife. She had missed her goal as a mother—she would not get another chance. The thought devastated her. She began to relive her past, analyzing what she could have done differently. Her despair increased. But she could not redo the past. She had wanted nothing more than to have her children and husband rise up and call her blessed. And she had wanted to hear her Lord say, "Well done, my good and faithful servant."

My heart ached for her. I could understand the longing of her heart. I, too, loved my sons.

She told me that her pain reminded her of what she had heard about heart attacks—dull, heavy, never ceasing. Like a boulder on her chest. Her heart had been raped, deprived of her son's love. The pain immobilized her . . . until she ran in prayer to her Father God, her Jehovah-Rapha.

Then God reminded her that he understood her desire for intimacy with her child. Some of His children had cut Him off, failing to spend time with Him, believing He had failed them.

"But, Father, You didn't fail," she almost yelled at Him, "I did."

And then, in answer to her anguish, that still, small voice came into her mind, "I know I did not fail, and I know that you are not perfect. But remember, I am greater than your failures. I am God, and I have promised you—and your son, whether he believes it or not—that all things will work together for good. He is mine and I will use it all to conform him into the image of my Son. Now, what are my promises? Believe them. Live by them. Do what I have taught you to do. Regardless of how your son responds, believe and obey me. You cannot redeem the past. I can. Walk in faith. Either my Word is true or it isn't and you know it is truth."

As my friend began to wrestle with whether her thoughts were simply what she wanted to hear or if they were from the Spirit, she told me with a chagrined look that she finally gave in. She knew that what had been in her heart was in accord with the Word of God and the character of God. The wrestling was over. Faith "pinned her to the mat."

How I rejoiced! Although her situation didn't change for a, long time, she was no longer incapacitated by her sorrow. She found her refuge, her Gilead, and there she dwells by faith.

—**Kay Arthur**

Jumping Fences

The first time God gave me a glimpse of my future I thought it was a weird notion I dreamt up myself. I was sixteen at the time, locked up in Juvenile Hall, awaiting a five-year sentence to California Youth Authority (CYA). No one knew how desperately I wanted to belong and be loved. I kept it hidden underneath a cold, hard exterior that screamed, *I don't need anyone. No one will ever hurt me again.*

After attending a few of the church services, which I primarily attended to see the male inmates, I wrestled with believing God could love me.

Late one evening I waited for my cellmate to fall asleep. I stood on my bed as I looked out our single window and cried into the night. "Dear God, please help me. Are You real? I don't have anyone."

There was nothing announcing that God heard me or even cared. So I climbed back down to my bed and cried myself to sleep.

The very next morning, "tough Lille" crawled out of bed, feeling the same. But the next time I went to church a lady came with a guitar and sang to us. Music and art were the only things that kept me interested in life. For an instant I saw myself on her side of the fence somewhere in the future helping others like myself find their way home. I felt crazy for allowing myself to entertain such a thought. *Who would want to hear anything I had to say or sing?* I buried the vision in a dark bag called rejection.

Many years later I discovered that God had been with me. In January, 1985, I repeated the same prayer I had prayed as a sixteen year old prisoner, "Please show me if You're real, God."

This time the Father answered me with the words I'd yearned to hear all my life. He said, "I love you. I've always loved you. I've been waiting for you."

I desperately tried to deny what I'd heard, but the love in His voice removed all my doubt. I'd been wooed like a moth to a flame, never realizing how cold I'd been until I surrendered to God's warmth.

That was eleven years ago. Today I am fulfilling the vision He placed in my heart to help others "over the fence." I travel all over the United States singing and sharing my story to numerous groups, churches, jails, Juvenile Halls, Interface, Foster Care programs and CYA.

Times have changed since I was locked up as a teenager. Today's troubled youth wear much heavier armor. Recently I was the guest speaker for a retreat for Interface teens, ages sixteen to eighteen. (Interface helps kids gain skills to face the world without drugs, alcohol and gangs.)

This particular group I was speaking to had chips on their shoulders thicker than concrete. After telling them about my own troubles as a teenager, I saw them begin to respond. I looked at each one in the group while I talked, taking care not to bring attention to anyone whose "hard guy" mask was beginning to slip off.

But not everyone responded well. Two of the boys in the group heckled me without mercy during the entire evening. Normally when I close my presentation, I ask each one to share their dreams from before they got in trouble. I was afraid the two rude dudes had intimidated the others to keep silent.

I prayed silently for a breakthrough. To my amazement, one of the verbally abusive boys wearing a stocking hat spoke up and announced he wanted to become a sheriff. We all cracked up in spontaneous laughter. He explained he wanted to know what it was to break the law so he could be a better law enforcer. Again, the room filled with laughter.

John, the other boy who was "chief heckler," answered, "I want to be a scientist and discover ways to rid the planet of pollution." He continued on for a few moments explaining what university he'd like to go to and ways he wanted to change the world to make it a better place. His face glowed while he talked. I was witnessing a lamb on his way to the other side of the fence.

As soon as the meeting ended, the future scientist put the hard guy mask back on and headed out the door to catch up with his girlfriend. I hurried to catch up with them.

"Thanks for letting me come tonight," I said.

"Yeah, well . . . thanks for coming," he said, softening just a little.

"You know, John, I fully expect to read about you in *Newsweek* in a few years."

"Why do you say that?" he asked, stunned.

"Because you have goals, a game plan, and that's how dreams become real."

As I walked to my car, I overheard him say to his girl, "Did you hear what she said? She told me she'd read about me in *Newsweek*! Wow!"

God fulfilled the vision He placed in my heart so long ago. I know the others who hide behind stony cold masks may very well cry out into the night asking God to show him if He's real. I know He will hold them as they cry themselves to sleep. Some may even remember me and have a strange vision of jumping over the fence to my side.

—Lille Diane

Chet

I met Chet Bitterman in 1978, on an administrative trip from Colombia to Wycliffe Bible Translators' International Linguistic Center in Dallas. I arranged a lunch with Chet and his wife, Brenda, who were planning to go to Colombia as translators. While they were both personable, they had no doubts about their call.

At the time, the Summer Institute of Linguistics (SIL) was having trouble getting visas in Colombia for our new workers. Members were going on furlough and short-term assistants were leaving because their terms were over. Our personnel situation was critical.

As we talked about that, Chet said, "Will, don't worry. God is leading Brenda and me to Colombia. He'll get us visas, and everyone else is going to get their visas, too!"

He also said, "Will, we're ready to do anything for God. We're willing to go to the hardest place. If there's something no one else wants to do, we'll do that."

His faith was real. He and Brenda did receive their resident visas by the time they finished their linguistics and Spanish studies. Many new members came with them, filling our ranks with good people.

The guerrilla movements in Colombia were focusing on our mission as one of their targets, using us to embarrass the government while making every effort to rid their country of "foreign imperialists." As conditions worsened, we took numerous security measures to protect our members.

In January, 1979, our branch conference passed a resolution saying that our branch wouldn't pay "ransom, blackmail or extortion." This was widely accepted because we realized that if we ever did, it would encourage further attempts against Wycliffe's work around the world.

Colombian military intelligence had warned us that up to 150 insurgents were planning to attack our isolated center of operations. Thirty soldiers were brought there to protect us. Tensions rose, and I advised our members that they could be transferred to a safer assignment. No one accepted.

As Chet and Brenda awaited their assignment, I asked Chet to serve as my assistant, handling security matters at our center, which he did enthusiastically. He and Brenda knew the potential danger. Unknown to me, Chet had said to Brenda previously, "I'd hate for any of our people to get hurt, but it'd be better to sacrifice a few lives if necessary than to give in to these jokers and encourage them to do it again."

Chet and Brenda made a brief trip to Bogota with their two daughters. Early January 19, 1981, the doorbell rang where they were staying. The house manager, seeing a uniform, assumed the visitor was a legitimate officer and opened the door. Armed masked men rushed through the door with the "officer."

The intruders put a newly-arrived member into their vehicle. Because he knew more Spanish, Chet began relating with the terrorists and intervened on behalf of the member, who was finally returned to the house. Instead, Chet was taken.

As they left, they threatened, "SIL must leave the country within one month, or we will kill this man."

I arrived in Bogota the next day to manage the crisis. I checked with our branch and international administrations concerning our response to the demands. We agreed that we couldn't leave the country to save Chet. Too much was involved.

Although some of our members disagreed with our decision, I was convinced Chet would say to me, "Will, I am where God put me. Don't be concerned for me. Remember what I told you in Dallas."

The media picked up the story, and over the weeks their tone went from being critical of our mission, to neutral and finally favor. One Catholic priest on his daily broadcast said: "If Chet Bitterman is killed, he'll be a martyr of the Church."

As negotiations continued, Chet was given permission to send a couple of letters. As a P.S. to one, he wrote: "Brenda, I have to tell you it is very important that you collaborate with my caplietors and that you should all believe Colombia." His obvious misspellings went unnoticed by his captors, but he again put his life on the line for what he believed in.

Then I received the fateful call one morning from the American embassy. "Chet's body has been found on a bus. He was shot. The police are investigating the report."

That same day, we flew him to our center and buried him in Colombia, where we knew he would want to be.

At the grave I told Chet, "You know I love and respect you. I did everything I knew to save you. I'm sorry I failed."

I could almost hear him tell me: "Don't forget that I volunteered to take any assignment no one else was willing to take. This was my calling."

Chet's death wasn't in vain. He bought SIL years of time and it is still working in Colombia. Many language programs have been completed; others are nearing completion. Chet's sacrifice kept the door open.

—Will Kindberg

Flying First Class

As I arrived at the airport for a cross-country trip, I received a pleasant surprise. Due to an abundance of frequent-flier miles, I had been granted a first-class upgrade on my flight.

I boarded the plane ahead of the crowd and was greeted by name. I settled into a wide and comfortable seat, in close proximity to the pilot. The food was excellent, and the service I received was graciously given.

However, the trip was not entirely smooth. Approximately halfway through the flight we encountered some rough weather. As I reflected on my situation, I realized that although being seated in first class did not exempt me from experiencing turbulence, it somehow made it easier to endure.

Perhaps flying in first class provides a glimpse of the benefits of abiding. When we choose to abide in Christ, it doesn't mean that we will escape hardship. However, as we stay close to Him, we will experience the inner calm of His indwelling presence. Instead of being overwhelmed with the turbulence of life, we will experience His grace, comfort, intimacy, and peace.

Traveling in first class is the most comfortable way to fly. Abiding in Christ is the most privileged way to live.

—**Cynthia Heald**

13

Loss Of A Child

Why are you downcast, O my soul? Why so disturbed within me? Put your hope in God, for I will yet praise him, my Savior and my God.

Psalm 42:11

Heaven Is A Bit Like Grandma's House

After our two-year-old son, Jamie, died, I was comforted by the knowledge that he was well cared for in heaven. But I worried that he had forgotten the mommy and daddy who loved him so much. Since there's no sadness in heaven, I reasoned, he can't miss us or worry about us.

Finally I asked my husband, Dwaine, "Do you think Jamie just forgot about us? Or does he wonder why we're not there enjoying the glories of heaven with him?"

Dwaine thought for awhile. "Try to look at it this way," he said. "Remember when we used to leave him with Grandma for a few hours? He'd kiss us good-bye, then hurry to Grandma's toy shelf. When we returned, he'd run to us with outstretched arms, happy to see us again."

I nodded, remembering our sturdy boy flinging himself at me full force when I stepped into my mother-in-law's house.

Dwaine continued. "But Grandma said he never cried for us while we were gone. He knew we always came back for him, and in the meantime he was perfectly content with Grandma and her sugar cookies and story books. Isn't that right?"

Yes, I had to admit, that was true. Grandma's house had been Jamie's favorite place to go.

"Well, I think that's how it is now," he finished gently, putting an arm around my shoulders. "Don't you imagine God surpasses even Grandma at keeping little boys happy and secure?"

I had to agree with that also. If I could trust my mother-in-law with him for a few hours, then I could trust God with him forever.

—Bonnie Hellum Brechbill

A Closetful Of Balloons

Somewhere up in heaven,
There's a closetful of balloons,
Each one carefully tagged and stored,
Awaiting its proper owner.
A rainbow of colors paying silent tribute,
To moments of joy and sorrow.
Though angels question the wisdom of such a collection,
They faithfully add each lost balloon as it arrives.
They do not understand, you see,
What an innocent child knows for sure,
That the God who stores up each one of our tears,
Knows the value of a child's balloon.

—Sandy Burgess

244 **GOD'S VITAMIN "C" FOR THE HURTING SPIRIT**

Forgiving God

There came a point after my son was killed by a drunk driver when I needed to forgive God. God in Himself never needs forgiveness, but there are times in our lives when from our point of view things look so unfair and so hurtful, that we need to say, "God, I forgive You. I don't understand. From my vantage point, it seems You really hurt me. I know You have a purpose, and You have the road map, but I don't. I can't always see Your plan, and from my point of view, it doesn't make a whole lot of sense." It is not sacrilegious to say, "God, I forgive You." It is an exercise we may need to go through to get back on speaking terms with God and acknowledge the severe pain we have gone through.

After Nathan's death, I also had to forgive myself. Perhaps you may have to go through that too, especially if you were involved in the incident which caused your pain. "Why didn't I see it coming? Why didn't I know? Why didn't I sense it?"

I wasn't with Nathan the night he was killed, so I kept thinking, *Why didn't I go to that basketball game with him?* Though I wouldn't have been riding with him if I had gone, it was different than normal that I didn't go. So I reasoned that must be why it happened. I failed. I wasn't a good parent that night. I didn't go to the basketball game.

I was a great parent, and I knew it at the time. But for a while, I kept thinking, *Why didn't I pay more attention? If I had known* . . . I finally had to say, "Marilyn, if there's anything you've done wrong, I forgive you." I had to look myself in the mirror and say, "I know you're a nice lady. I know you love Nathan. You did everything you could. If you made mistakes, I forgive you."

There was yet another person I had to forgive. I went through a day of prayer and emotional healing with a group called Philippians Ministries.

I spent a morning talking through my life. Then in the afternoon the prayer director worked with me and we prayed through different situations. I talked with God about significant people in my life and asked forgiveness for wrong things I had done toward them. During this time the director asked if I would tell God that I forgive Nathan for dying.

I just about jumped out of my chair. I said, "It wasn't his fault!"

She said, "I know that, but can you forgive him for dying?"

"Well, of course, because it wasn't his fault?"

She said, "Fine. Why don't you say that to God?"

I tried to say it, but I couldn't get it out. It took me a long time. I sat there and cried and prayed. Finally, the first words that came out were, "Nate, why'd you leave me so soon?" I realized I was mad at him. I know that's not logical, but I can guarantee some of you are also mad at an innocent party, You may be thinking, *Couldn't you have noticed the danger? Couldn't you sense you were in trouble? Couldn't you have done something different? Couldn't you have prevented the divorce? Why didn't you try harder to please the boss so you wouldn't lose your job? You shouldn't have risked our money on those bad investments. Why didn't you take better care of yourself? You should have noticed that lump sooner.*

Many times, as I went down the freeway, I would look at the exit Nate took the night of the accident, and I think, *Nate, why didn't you take Waterman instead of Del Rosa? Couldn't you have done better? Couldn't you see that car coming? Why didn't you get there a little sooner or a little later?* All of those things may seem silly now, yet I needed to release my feelings and admit there was something that made me mad at Nate, even though I loved him and would have given my life for him.

—Marilyn Willett Heavilin

Two White Roses

I was called to the phone Wednesday morning while teaching at Kids' Day Out to speak with my daughter, Andrea, in Dallas. "Mother," she began, "Amber is at the doctor's office, her sonogram was this morning. They discovered twins." She spoke about her sister, my daughter, and her voice sounded pained.

I had only one second to be excited. "Mother," she continued, her voice breaking, "They are both dead. Amber is very upset. They paged Donny and he is on his way there. I have her children at my house and knew you would want to be praying."

Leaning against the wall, I softly wept as I prayed for my daughter and her family. Returning to my classroom, I encountered ten beautiful toddlers running, laughing and playing. In that moment, I wanted to gather all of them in my arms to feel their warmth.

Later in the day, I spoke with Amber and learned that a surgical procedure was planned that would prepare her body for the removal of the four-month-old fetuses later in the week. It all seemed so sterile, so cold, and yet, necessary. Together we grieved.

Friday morning, I was awakened by the ringing phone. Donny's voice blurted out, "Mom, we're at the hospital. It's over, but because of low blood pressure, Amber is in surgery."

Clutching the receiver to my breast, I silently sang, "Jesus loves me this I know, for the Bible tells me so, little ones to Him belong, they are weak but He is strong."

Later in the day I was able to talk with Amber. "Mom, what do you think of having a graveside service?"

I instantly agreed, promising that if they made that decision, we would be there. We talked about the impact that this loss was having on six-year-old Michael and three-year-old Rebekah. They were actively aware of the pregnancy and now experienced a great loss. They had big questions to ask about what would happen to the babies. For them, for all of us, this closure was needed and sacred.

We learned Amber had been carrying identical twin boys. We mused about how hectic her life would have been!

"Amber, you may want to name the babies," I suggested.

"Why?" She sounded surprised.

"Well, Scripture says God calls us by name."

She agreed to discuss it with Donny.

Donny located a cemetery in Lewisville that has a special section for babies. It was here that they decided to place their sons.

On March 31, 1996, Palm Sunday, we attended the graveside service. I stood there gazing at a small white satin coffin, surrounded by beautiful flowers and sets of blue teddy bears. Tucked inside, forever to be remembered on this day, were my grandsons, Chad and Nathan Fulton. Close church friends, grandparents, great-grandparents, aunts and uncles, came to support Donny, Amber and the children. And there was love, lots of love.

My grief was enlarged as my thoughts traveled back to a previous Palm Sunday in 1965. Ironically, over thirty years before, in my fourth month of pregnancy, I too experienced this loss. I named the child Jennifer, placed her in a small white box and buried her on our farm in Nebraska. Though other children came after her, including Amber, I still remember that Palm Sunday and my special angel.

The statement made by our family that day at a graveside service stands as a monument to our faith and belief. Chad and Nathan were real little boys, meticulously formed in Amber's womb, precious in God's sight. Though many babies are aborted in the fourth month and tossed aside, we do not regard them as "tissue" to be discarded. As time passes and other grandchildren join our family, the story will be told, the grave visited. I am convinced that this will be a reminder to all of our family that life is sacred.

We said our good-byes in Dallas and returned to Kansas City and our responsibilities there. On Tuesday, I returned to work.

Kristy came in that day to pick up her son, Christian, who was in my care. She was unable to conceal her large protruding tummy, for inside she carried twin boys. In her hands she carried two perfect white roses. Without a word, she placed them on my lap. The card read, "In memory of Chad and Nathan, God's special angels." And though she had not met Amber, she grieved for her all day long. My heart was touched and warmed. We grieved together.

The phone rang. Exciting news! Kristy's twins, Brady and Perry have arrived. Come, hold them, was the invitation. I shall go today; my heart will be blessed and healed.

—Judith A. Wiegman

Passport To Heaven

I stood there stunned. My twenty-nine-year-old daughter, Sally, had received the test results. Melanoma cancer! Three to six months to live.

"Oh, God," I breathed, "Please not our Sally." But in my heart I knew it was true. No parent expects or is prepared to lose a child in death. It's just not the proper order of life.

Sally decided against chemotherapy and chose to follow a natural food and enzyme therapy. She moved home with us, yet continued to work full time. Her boss and co-workers went together and sent her and her married sister, Nancy, on a two-week trip to Hawaii. She came home tanned and beautiful. She looked anything but ill.

Three months passed, then six. Sally still looked great and worked four or five days a week. Her friends supported and encouraged her. I continued to prepare the meals on her natural food diet.

That February, Sally celebrated her 30th birthday. At the end of one year she returned to the doctor. He showed surprise and said, "Sally, I don't know what you are doing, but keep it up!" We were encouraged but after the examination the doctor reported liver enlargement and that the cancer was still slowly growing.

Four months later, Sally felt too weak to continue working. She continued to attend church and a weekly Bible Study and prayed for a miraculous healing. We knew she had been drawn closer to God over the last year. I thought back to the night when she'd asked Jesus to come into her life. She was only ten—so many years ago. I remembered the warm feeling I had when I prayed with her.

Sally began to lose weight rapidly. Her eyes and mouth seemed too big for her face. I longed to hold her on my lap again as I had when she was little.

Eighteen months after the doctor's first verdict, we put up a hospital bed in our home. Sally could hardly get out of her own low bed. She was up with help during the day. She still loved to eat and looked forward to meals.

That last night we helped her to bed. At 2:30 a.m. her Dad got her some ice chips to chew. I asked, "Is there anything else you need?"

"I don't think so," she answered with a little girl lilt in her voice, as she flashed us a radiant smile. She never woke up again. Since, I've wondered if she had glimpsed heaven.

In a blur the visitation and funeral came and went. I couldn't sleep. In my numb mind I kept hearing Sally ring the tiny blue dinner bell she used to call me during the night. If I dropped off to sleep I'd awake in a cold sweat.

I thought of other mothers who'd lost a child. I even thought of Mary, Jesus' Mother, and what she felt losing her Son in his thirties. As a mother, Mary must have felt the same emptiness I did.

The first months were hard. So many reminders—her empty chair at the table, magazines and letters delivered in the mail, occasional phone calls, fixing meals she had enjoyed, seeing clothes in her favorite color, purple. And then there was her little dog. For weeks after she died, Zac searched everywhere for her.

Yet other things comforted me and I learned to hum the tune, "The Joy of the Lord is Our Strength" when I was sad. He truly was my strength through those months.

At last the lonely ache subsided. Finally I knew I must go through Sally's personal papers. When I found her passport, it fell open to the page with the picture of her happy smiling face. It blurred as I studied it. I started to throw it in the waste-basket—then the thought filled me, "Sally had her passport to Heaven!" I brushed away my tears and smiled as I tried to imagine her arrival at her destination; the joy she must have felt on meeting Jesus and the people from the Bible stories she had learned as a child. Also meeting her grandparents and great-grandparents must have been exciting.

It's still hard to realize I won't see our lovely daughter again here on earth; but I need to learn to say, when asked about my three living children, "And I also have another daughter, Sally, who lives in Heaven."

As I ponder what she is doing now, I can joyfully smile. But I must ask, "Is *your* Passport to Heaven in order?"

—Mary Lou Klingler

In Remembrance Of Jamie

God hath bountifully given
And God hath taken away.
What aches fill the hearts
of the parents who part
With the joy of their life this way.

God gave us a son—our first-born.
He filled our days with light.
Now our child is gone,
his short life is done,
And our souls have been plunged into night.

What hope is there for the morrow
When death has claimed our joy?
We cling to this only:
though life is so lonely,
Some day we'll again see our boy.

He brightened our lives for a moment.
Surely now he plays near the Throne.
And some day we'll see him
run happy and free
In Heaven, his lovely new home.

"Jamie, God's plans were different.
He, too, strove to give you the best.
So into His keeping while you were yet sleeping
Your sweet soul was laid on His breast."

We think of God's throne up in Heaven,
Where the saints at His feet in praise lay.
We think of the love and the joy there,
And we know we'll see Jamie some day.

— Lynell Gray

Count Your Blessings

My young friend, Tommy, suffered with cystic fibrosis. When he was eight and not doing well, his doctors hospitalized him again. Tommy was a trooper, not complaining about his bedridden days. Finally, however, his doctors allowed him to take a walk outside around the hospital, his mother Meralea towing his portable oxygen unit behind them.

As they made their way from the fourth floor to the lobby, Meralea was painfully aware of bystander's reactions. Most offered her pitying glances and Tommy's mom began to feel very sorry about her son's situation.

"Not only was I feeling sorry for Tommy, but myself as well," she says.

Excited about his trip outdoors, Tommy hadn't noticed anyone's sympathy. He continued on around the hospital, his slippers making a "plop-plop" rhythm on the sidewalk as he walked.

"Mom," he said, smiling up at his mother. "Guess what song my slippers make me think of?"

"What song, Tommy?" Meralea asked, her mind still on her problems.

Not missing a beat, Tommy sang with his footsteps, "Count your blessings, name them one by one. Count your blessings, see what God has done . . . ."

Meralea joined in on the chorus. Tommy's song helped her count her blessings, not burdens. Now that her son has gone to be with the Lord, Meralea considers that stroll around the hospital one of her most precious memories.

—Cynthia Culp Allen

When The Pieces Don't Fit

I quietly wiped unexpected tears as the doctor asked how I was. Though I determined to "appear" collected, his gentle concern stirred a mixture of emotions within my heart. It had been just a few weeks since we'd discovered I was pregnant with our third child. Our four and a-half-year-old, Elisabeth, enthusiastically announced to everyone that "Laura Louise" was in Mommy's tummy. Her cheerful Crayola art of our growing family covered the refrigerator door; each stick figure proudly wearing a smile from ear-to-ear as a tiny "stick baby" grinned from Mommy's tummy. Our two-year-old son, T.J., processed the news with greater reserve. Periodically he would lift my shirt and poke my abdomen to locate "the baby." Confident it was there somewhere, he frequently thanked the Lord in our evening prayer time for the "baby inside Mommy."

Amid the growing excitement, subtle aches and pains stirred quiet concerns within me. Now, as the doctor stood alongside the examining table, the image on the ultrasound monitor was motionless. So many emotions flooded my heart as I anxiously scanned the screen—hopeful that the shadow would stir, yet numb from the stillness that was before me. Unable to embrace the transition from hope to hurt, delight to disappointment, I watched, silent, teary, and inwardly alone as I began to say good-bye to the hopes and dreams this little one represented.

My mind was clouded as I made my way from the office to the adjoining lawn where Elisabeth and T.J. waited with their Dad. Briefly, I shared that there was a problem with the baby and that it wouldn't be coming to join our family after all. Elisabeth's sobs broke painfully into the air as Ted and I quietly wiped our tears while making our way to the car.

Driving home, an engulfing silence seemed to grip each of us, no one knowing quite what to say. The silence was broken by the gentle voice of little T.J. from his car seat. With a quiet confidence, he stated, "The little baby was sick, Mommy, and went to be with God. He's the only one that could love on it." A lump in my throat kept me from responding but as we shared a gaze, there was a sense that God indeed would care for each of us, even the little one we lost.

The reality of the loss lingers, as well as the heartfelt desire to have held and known this little one. It has been a season of experiences that has brought with it a sense that somehow, even when the fragmented pieces of life can't be made to fit, that God will give us peace; and give us a quiet assurance that He will walk with us through this experience.

—Patty Stump

Cradled In His Arms

The operating room was freezing. My body shook as nurses solemnly went about their duties, strapping me down to the table for emergency surgery. With my eyes no-where to look but upwards, the brilliant lights formed haloes as my vision blurred and tears gathered.

"Mrs. Ling, I need you to count backwards, starting with ten," instructed the anesthesiologist.

There was urgency in his voice as he repeated, "Mrs. Ling, please begin counting, now."

Before I started, I begged the surgeon, "We want to have children, please do whatever you can."

His warm eyes assured me he would give me his best.

"Ten, nine, eight," my speech began to slur and I silently prayed for God's protection. "Seven, six, five. . . " My thoughts were spinning like a whirlwind and my mind relived recent events as darkness veiled the room.

We were a statistic. One out of five couples have trouble conceiving or are infertile. After nine years of marriage, I had my first positive pregnancy test. We were elated. Our phone bill sky rocketed. The nurse scheduled my first prenatal visit three long weeks away. With out-of-town vacation plans, I knew time would pass by quickly. I could hardly wait to visit my obstetrician.

Things went great until the morning of July 14. I experienced extreme abdominal pain, hemorrhaged, and my temperature soared. We made frantic phone calls and upon instruction by my obstetrician, I was rushed to an emergency room, 300 miles from home.

After several hours filled with examinations, ultrasounds, and concerned looks from attending physicians, we were finally informed I had lost the baby. My condition was life-threatening and I needed emergency surgery.

Even though a curtain was all that separated my husband and

me from the emergency room filled with patients and medical personnel, it seemed empty as we found solitude in our little cubicle. We clung to each other and sobbed as our hopes and dreams of a little one were snatched from our very arms. Our grief for the one we would never cradle here on earth began that very moment.

Our love grew deeper as we began to pick up the pieces. We thanked God for a successful surgery and the encouraging news that chances were good for another pregnancy.

Nothing prepared me for the emotions that surfaced after the loss of our baby. Kind souls that tried to lighten our pain with expressions like, "You're young, you can have more," "It was for the best," or "Just be thankful you were only a few months along," rubbed salt in my open, wounded heart. Days were filled with silence and misunderstanding. Cards and phone calls were a wonderful blessing and comfort, but we grieved alone. Yet, God drew me closer to Him through the isolation.

Knowing my open wound would eventually heal, I determined that when I heard of a couple who had lost a child, I would mourn with them, and let them know it is natural to grieve. I wanted to communicate that they were not alone in this heart-wrenching journey.

God answers prayers. Over the years, time-and-time again, in that deep corner of my heart, pain and grief emerge when I hear of someone's loss of a child. As I've done many times, I track down their address, write them an encouraging note, offer my sympathy and prayers, and send them one of my favorite books on the subject, *Free To Grieve* by Maureen Rank (Bethany House).

Life is a learning process. When faced to walk the lonely and tragic death of an unborn child, so dearly wanted and loved, I knew I could turn to God, who truly knows all the emotions and pain of death and losing a Son. Even though my arms ached to hold my baby, I felt the warmth of God's love as He cradled me in His arms. He held me tight as I gained renewed strength to carry on with empty arms. Which, by the way, God eventually filled when, two years later, I, again, was in an operating room. This time I was able to cradle a scrunched up, little-faced, squirmy, healthy baby boy, known to the world as Philip.

—Georgia Curtis Ling

Contributors

Deborah Kaye Adamo is a working housewife and free-lance writer. Her poetry has appeared in many publications including *The Other Side of Midnight* (The National Library of Poetry) and *Treasured Poems of America*. Contact: 198 Tecumseh St., St. Charles, MO 63301. (314) 947-9057.

Charlotte Adelsperger is the author of two books and numerous articles and poetry published in *Decision*, *Virtue*, *Teachers in Focus* and other publications. She speaks to groups and has led writers' workshops in five states. She is married to Bob and has two grown children. Contact: 11629 Riley, Overland Park, KS 66210. (913) 345-1678.

Cynthia Culp Allen, winner of two Amy Writing Awards, has published over 300 articles in newspapers, books, and magazines. She is the author of *Home Is Where You Hang Your Heart* and *More Encouraging Than Flowers* (Meridian Publishing). Contact: P.O. Box 214, Corning, CA 96021. (916) 824-0980.

Eunice Ann Badgley is a mother, grandmother, widow, and graduate of Park College, Parkville, MO. She enjoys reading, writing, crafts, and the country. Eunice Ann has several short articles published. Contact: 451 Spring Avenue, Liberty, MO 64068. (816) 781-8908.

Gwen Bagne was widowed in April, 1994, at the age of 44. She has two married sons and attends the Northwest Foursquare Church in Federal Way. She speaks at workshops on grief. Contact: P.O. Box 52, Milton, WA 98354. (253) 874-5082.

Vickie Baker is a free-lance writer, co-facilitates a class on Attendant Care, has a penpal prison ministry, and has given her testimony several times. She is working on her first book, *Surprised by Hope*. Contact: 2215 S. Decatur, Denver, CO 80219. (303) 934-7476.

Venus E. Bardanouve, a retired speech pathologist, has published many Christian articles, as well as Bible study guides and a book, *Monologues for Ministry*. She was granted an honorary doctorate from Montana State University in May, 1996. Contact: P.O. Box 367, Harlem, MT 59526. (406) 353-2397.

Mildred Barger attends the Phoenix Christian Writers group and is a former co-leader of Bethany Writers. She has authored numerous articles, several books, and has taught workshops on writing devotions.

Christine Barrett is a Bible teacher, speaker for women's groups, and free-lance writer. She has prepared stories and teaching materials for teachers and children for 25 years as a director of Child Evangelism Fellowship. Contact: 2325 Cole St., East Peoria, IL 61611.

Delores Elaine Bius has sold over 1,700 articles and stories in 25 years of writing. She is an instructor for American Christian Writers and speaks at conferences and retreats. Delores is a widow and mother of five grown sons. Contact: 6400 So. Narragansett Ave., Chicago, IL 60638. (773) 586-4384.

Dr. Lorrie Boyd is a professional speaker, retreat leader, and co-author of the book, *Change Your Life With Humor*. Lorrie speaks on "The Healing Power of Prayer and Play" and "Healing Grief and Loss with the Spirit of Play." Contact: 12555 Euclid St. Suite 25, Garden Grove, CA 92640. (714)636-5457.

Bonnie Hellum Brechbill has been published in *Newsweek*, *New York Newsday*, *Highlights for Children* and many other magazines and newspapers. She has won writing awards from *Writer's Digest* and *Byline*. She lives on a dairy farm with her husband and daughter. Contact: 8778 Edenville-Cheesetown Rd, Chambersburg, PA 17201-9543.

Jan Brunette is the mother of four, the stepmother of seven, and the grandmother of fifteen. Her articles have appeared in *The Lutheran Witness*, *Evangelizing Today's Child*, and many other publications. Jan has taught in Christian schools for twelve years. Contact 2711 Bayview Dr., Eustis, FL 32726.

Sandy Burgess is a speaker/writer who teaches from her heart of compassion with a gift of encouragement. Her insights and humor inspire others to seek God's presence in their own lives. Contact: 7915 East Longfellow, Spokane, WA 99212.

Penny Carlevato has been married to Norm for 34 years and has three grown children and five grandchildren. She is a Registered Nurse working in Outpatient Surgery and teaches children's Sunday School. Penny is very involved in women's ministry and shares a passion of tea as an outreach ministry. Contact: 714 Bungalow Dr., El Segundo, CA 90245. (310) 640-2190.

Jeri Chrysong has been published in various devotional books, as well as *God's Vitamin "C" for the Spirit* and *God's Vitamin "C" for the Christmas Spirit*. She also writes commentaries and opinions for newspapers, and is a poet. Jeri is a legal secretary and lives with her two sons in Huntington Beach, CA.

Doris C. Crandall, a free-lance inspirational writer, has been published in more than two dozen religious and inspirational magazines including *Christian Education Today*, *Guideposts* magazine and anthologies, and *The Lutheran Digest*. Contact: 2303 Victoria Street, Amarillo, TX 79106.

Teresa Daniels, an encourager and creative communicator for over 25 years, enjoys teaching the Word. She speaks, sings, and writes for her church, seminars, conferences, and women's events. She also trains small group leaders through The Women's Ministries Institute. Contact: 3502 W. Magill Ave. Fresno, CA 93711. (209) 438-0176.

Danna Demetre, RN, is a writer, motivational speaker, and founder of LifeStyle Dimensions, whose passion is to encourage individuals toward a life of greater balance. She has over 20 years experience in the medical and fitness fields and was a corporate marketing manager and professional trainer. Contact: 3111 Camino del Rio North, Suite 203, San Diego, CA 92018. (619) 528-0777.

Denise A. DeWald is a writer whose works have appeared in *The Upper Room*, Regular Baptist Press, Barbour Books, etc. Some of her poems have been made into songs, one of which has been aired on Family Life Radio. Contact: 1744 Swenson Road, Au Gres, MI 48703. (517) 876-8718.

Lille Diane has inspired thousands nationwide with her personal story and concert, "From Ashes to Beauty." Lille's refreshing speaking style combines humor, music and exhortation. Contact: P.O. Box 924, Oak View, CA 93022. (805) 649-1805.

Gloria H. Dvorak has been married for 38 years and has three children and four grandchildren. She started to write in 1989 and has about 80 articles published. Gloria has previous experience as a production manager of a travel magazine in New York City and as a secretary at advertising agencies.

David Evans is a free-lance poet with a number of published poems. He is an estimator for an electrical contracting company. Dave enjoys church, reading, hiking, and riding and training his Arabian gelding, Dillon. Contact: 4162 Fireside Circle, Irvine, CA 92604-2216. (714) 551-5296.

Marjorie K. Evans is a free-lance writer of many articles and a former teacher. She enjoys grandparenting, reading, church work, traveling, her Welsh Corgi, and tending plants. She and husband, Edgar, have two sons and five grandchildren. Contact: 4162 Fireside Circle, Irvine, CA 92604-2216. (714) 551-5296.

Florence Ferrier and her husband, Darwin, live near Baudette, in Northern Minnesota. She is a former social worker and now does volunteer work in addition to free-lance writing. Her work has appeared in over 40 magazines plus other publications.

Jo Franz is a free-lance writer and conference speaker, sharing God's love, hope and joy in a ministry of word and song. Contact: 82 Sandcastle, Aliso Viejo, CA 92656. (714) 362-5545.

Mary Bahr Fritts has authored juvenile titles, *The Memory Box, Jordi's Run* and soon-to-be-released, *The Boy Who Loved Snowflakes.* Winner of nine writing awards, she has published 125+ stories, columns, reviews and articles. Contact: 807 Hercules Place, Colorado Springs, CO 80906. (719) 630-8244.

Lynell Gray has been married for 27 years to her college sweetheart, Steve. They have three children. Lynell is a second grade teacher, and author of a chapter in a professional book for educators on the Theory of Multiple Intelligencies. Contact: 2867 Balfore Street, Riverside, CA 92506. (909) 788-2638.

Verda Glick and her family continue to serve as missionaries in El Salvador. God kept them safe through a war, kidnapping, and numerous armed robberies. Difficult experiences have stretched Verda's faith and led her to lean hard on God.

Bonnie Compton Hanson is a former editor with Scripture Press and co-author of three books. She enjoys free-lancing (over 375 manuscripts sold the last year and a-half), gardening and grandmothering.

Marilyn J. Hathaway is a retired RN, BSN. As a free-lance writer, she has been published in many Christian periodicals and local and state newspapers. Her favorite subject is "God Sightings"—finding God at work in the marketplace. Contact: 2101 Mariyana Ave., Gallup, NM 87901. (505) 722-9795.

Barbara Benedict Hibschman is a pastor's wife, mother, former missionary to the Philippines, and teacher. She is a speaker, author of 8 books, over 200 articles and poems, and contributing author to 8 devotional books. Contact: 326 Alexandria Way, Basking Ridge, NJ 07920. (908) 647-5745.

Mona Gansberg Hodgson is the author of the children's series *Desert Critter Adventures* (Concordia). She directs the Glorietta Christian Writers' Conference in New Mexico and speaks for women's retreats, MOPS, and other groups. Contact: P.O. Box 999, Cottonwood, AZ 86326-0999. Email: mona@sedona.net.

T.A. Huggins is married and the mother of two daughters. She is the adult ministries director of Merrillville First Church of the Nazarene. She is also currently employed as an anatomy and physiology instructor at Ivy Tech State College of Valparaiso, Indiana. Contact: 9519 Mckinley St., Crown Point, IN 46307. (219) 663-82832.

Betty Huff writes short devotionals, poems, and true stories. She has been published in *Catholic Digest* and her diocesan paper, *The Observer*. Contact: 10025 El Camino, #25, Atascadero, CA 93422. (805) 461-5619.

Jerry Jenkins, writer-in-residence for the Moody Bible Institute of Chicago, is the author of more than 100 books, including the bestsellers, *Left Behind* and *Tribulation Force*. He is a frequent guest on Focus on the Family radio program. He lives with his wife and boys at Three Son Acres, west of Zion, Illinois.

Will Kindberg served 38 years with Wycliffe Bible Translators as a Bible translator in the jungles of Peru and as an administrator in Colombia, where he faced terrorist threats. He writes about his experiences. Contact: 17261 Gothard St. #36, Huntington Beach, CA 92647. (714) 842-0303.

Mary Lou Klingler raised four children, is an R.N. and free-lance writer. Howard is her husband of 50 years. She founded and co-led a Christian writers' club for 15 years. Contact: 300 North Drive, Paulding, OH 45879-1025. (419) 399-3089 (Summer); 1056 E. Pueblo Rd. Phoenix, AZ 85020-4120. (602) 944-9479 (Winter).

Patty Kolb is a professional speaker for church, social, and youth organizations on a variety of subjects including trust, courage, suffering, and disability awareness. She is Ms. Wheelchair California 1997-1998 and is a graduate of C.L.A.S.S. (Christian Leaders, Authors, and Speakers Seminar). Her family resides in Carlsbad, CA Contact: (760) 753-8875.

Karen Kosman was born in Hollywood in 1942. Her life is full as a wife, mother, and grandmother of 13. Together with her husband, John, Karen has a drama and speaking ministry. Contact: P.O. Box 1507, La Mirada CA 90637-1507. (714) 941-2855.

Tina Krause is an award-winning newspaper columnist, free-lance writer, speaker, wife, mother of two grown sons and grandmother. She has over 600 published columns, articles, stories, and editorials in many magazines such as *Parents of Teenagers*, *Mature Years*, and *Sports Spectrum*. Contact: 223 Abington St., Valparaiso, IN 46385. (219) 531-2729.

Marilyn Krebs is a free-lance writer, originally from California where she and Marjie, the heroine of her story, grew up. She and her husband recently retired from ministry where she tutors and works in a hospital gift shop. Contact: 106 Bluefield Road, Starr, SC 29684. (864) 296-3732.

Marcia Krugh Leaser is a free-lance Christian writer who has been writing and submitting her work for some twenty years. Her many poems and articles have appeared in such magazines as: *Ideals, Decisions, Standard,* and many others. Her song ministry includes a wide variety of her original songs and poems. Contact: 2613 C. R. 118 Fremont, OH 43420. (419) 992-4307.

Georgia Curtis Ling is an entertaining speaker, writer and newspaper columnist who shares about faith, love and life. She is published in numerous magazines, and newspapers. This is her fourth contribution to a *God's Vitamin "C" for the Spirit* book. Contact: 4716 W. Glenhaven Drive, Everett, WA 98203. (425) 257-0377.

Helen Luecke is an inspirational writer of short stories, articles, and devotionals. She helped organize Inspirational Writers Alive!/Amarillo Chapter. Contact: 2921 S. Dallas, Amarillo, TX 79103. (806) 376-9671.

Carole Mayhall and her husband, Jack, work with The Navigators in the field of marriage, giving seminars nationally and overseas. Carole has written seven books and co-written two with Jack. She also frequently speaks at women's retreats. Contact: 5720 Velvet Court, Colorado Springs, CO 80918. (719) 534-9999; FAX: (719) 534-9490.

Janet McCracken, her husband Niel, and two children attend Rolling Hills Covenant Church. She is President and founder of the American Business Achievement Institute, a traing and consulting corporation in Torrance, CA. Contact: (301) 618-0222.

Ruth E. McDaniel began writing professionally in 1991 following an early retirement from an administrative position to care for her sick husband. She has received over 700 acceptances and 205 awards, and written two books. Her work has appeared in *Saturday Evening Post, Mature Living, Radar* and others.

Robertson McQuilkin is a homemaker, conference speaker, and writer. He is the author of four books and father of five living children, two of whom are missionaries. Robertson served 22 years as president of Columbia International University until his resignation in 1990 to care for his wife, Muriel.

Kathy Collard Miller is the best selling author of the *God's Vitamin "C" for the Spirit* series with her husband, Larry. The author of 29 books, she is also a popular speaker both nationally and internationally. Contact: P.O. Box 1058, Placentia, CA 92871. (714) 993-2654.

Elaine Munyan is a wife and mother of eight. She enjoys reading, writing, cooking and playing the piano. Elaine has homeschooled for seven years and studied music therapy at the University of Kansas. Contact: 9443 Connell Dr. Overland Park, KS 66212. (913) 541-8256.

Janie Ness is married to Doug and has three teenage children. As a homemaker, she places high value on family. She visits her parents regularly who still live in the childhood home bought shortly after a fire in 1960. Contact: 11118 N.E. 124th Ave., Vancouver, WA 98682. (360) 256-9304.

Jan Northington is a free-lance writer and conference speaker. She is the author of *Separated and Waiting* and has written numerous articles for the Christian marketplace. She is a wife and mother of four children. Contact: 2130 Sombrero Dr., Los Osos, CA 93402. (805) 528-2522.

Karen O'Connor is an award-winning author/speaker known for her inspiring books and presentations on intimacy in relationship. Karen has appeared on national radio and television and leads women's retreats. Contact: 2050 Pacific Beach Drive, #205, San Diego, CA 92109. (619) 483-3184.

Susan Titus Osborn is Editor of *The Christian Communicator*. She is an adjunct professor at Pacific Christian College. Susan has authored 12 books and is an author's representative for Broadman & Holman Publishers. She is married to Dick. Contact: 3133 Puente Street, Fullerton, CA 92835. (714) 990-1532.

Pat Palau and her husband, international evangelist Luis Palau, live in Portland, Oregon. They have extensive speaking and writing ministries, including contributing several chapters to *Keeping Your Kids Christian* (Servant Publications) and co-authoring the booklet *How to Lead Your Child to Christ* (Multnomah Press).

Lila Peiffer is the author of two novels, *The Secrets of the Roses* and *Rosehaven*. She's also appeared in a previous *God's Vitamin "C" for the Spirit*. Lila speaks for conferences on relationships and grief recovery. Contact: P.O. Box 966, Lake Arrowhead, CA 92352. (909) 337-1868.

Nancy E. Peterson has been a Christian writer and cartoonist for ten years. Her work has appeared in publications including *Housewife-Writer's Forum*, *The Press Enterprise*, and *the Inland Empire Christian Writer's Guild Newsletter*. She was founding editor of *The Bundy Canyon Christian Church Newsletter*.

Lois Erisey Poole is married to Robert. She has been writing for 20 years and has been published extensively throughout North America. She has just completed her first book, *Ring Around The Moon*. Contact: P.O. Box 3402, Quartz Hill, CA 93586-0402. (800) 476-5728.

Kayleen J. Reusser has published religious, travel, how-to, essay, profile, and business articles in *Decision*, *Today's Christian Woman*, *The Christian Reader*, *Grit*, and *Business People*. She is married to John and has three children. Contact: 1524 N. Sutton Cir. Bluffton, IN 46714. (219) 824-8573.

Laura Sabin Riley is a free-lance writer and homemaker. She has been published in *Decision* magazine and *God's Vitamin "C" for the Spirit*, and is in the process of writing a devotional book for stay-at-home moms. Contact: 10592 Del Vista Dr., Yuma, AZ 85367. (520) 342-7324.

Jean Rodgers is a self employed writer of promotional pieces, wrote a newspaper column, "We Women," for ten years, and has dozens of published essays. She's been married to John for 40 years and is the mother of four and grandmother to six. Contact: 2253 Elizabeth Dr., Broadview, IL 60153. (708) 681-4294.

Glenda Smithers has taught for 28 years. She authored *Out of Darkness*, a children's book (Nazarene) and writes curriculum and poetry. A workshop speaker, Glenda has two grandsons and lives in the country with her husband and many animals. Contact: 1875 N.W. 600 Rd. Kingsville, MO 64061. (816) 697-3990.

Rich Sprenkel, Jr. can be found running in races or behind his easel signing water color paintings. Rich stays busy maintaining a swimming pool business while finishing his bachelors degree at Chico State. Contact: P.O. Box 1754, Chico CA 95973. (916) 345-5440.

Martha Denlinger Stahl is a retired school teacher. She and her husband served as missionaries in Germany for four years. She has written articles, stories, and two Herald Press books, *Real People* and *By Birth or By Choice*. She resides in Lancaster, PA.

Ina C. Strain is a former missionary to Vietnam, a staff member of Radio Kids Bible Club, author of two books, and has written articles and devotionals published in both secular and Christian magazines. She began her free-lance writing at 82 years of age and currently lives with her daughter and family in Edison, NJ.

Patty Stump enjoys speaking at women's retreats, marriage seminars, Bible studies and special church events. She is also a wife, Christian counselor, free-lance writer, and full time mom to T.J. and Elisabeth. Contact: P.O. Box 5003, Glendale, AZ 85312. (602) 938-1460.

Doris Hays Toppen is a free-lance writer published in national magazines, a creative writing teacher and speaker. She enjoys biking, hiking, and camping with her four children, five grandchildren and their families. She lives at the foot of Mt. Si in Washington. Contact: 502 Janet Ave., NE, North Bend, WA 98045. (206) 888-0372.

Sherry Karuza Waldrip, an author/speaker/instigator, loves using humor to encourage women on a variety of topics. She is the author of *I Don't Remember Signing Up for Cancer!* Contact: E. 9116 Sprague Ave., Suite 139, Spokane, WA 99206. (509) 924-8085; (800) 395-8575. Email: SKaruza@aol.com

C. Ellen Watts is "Over 60" columnist for *Herald of Holiness* and writes prolifically for the Sunday school take-home market. Author of four books, she recently co-authored *Only One Life . . . the Autobiography of Lorraine O. Shultz* (Nazarene). Contact: 702 Alderwood Ln., Nampa, ID 83651.

Jerry L. Weaver has been an architect, author, college professor and dean. Since a debilitating stroke in 1994, he turned to making hand-carved drums which are sold in art galleries. He is recognized as a national Very Special Artist for the Kennedy Center. Contact: RR 2 Box 52, Lewis, KS 67552. (316) 659-3253.

Judith A. Wiegman is a storytelling speaker, singer, and writer. She shares her renewed life after divorce. She and her husband are ministers.

Judi, mother of 8 children, is available for retreats, seminars and workshops. Contact: 308 Brittany, Olathe, KS 66061. (913) 828-3857.

Cheryl L. Williams has devoted her life to helping others overcome adversities through her passionate belief in God and His love of all people. She's sought prudence and productivity in American humanitarian affairs. In 1990, she formed Project Share and Granny's Ink.

Sharon Wilkins is a speaker and an early childhood educator of 25 years. Her book, *Ready for Kindergarten*, helps parents and teachers prepare children for success. Sharon is married and has two daughters. Contact: 1157 W. Peninsula Dr., Gilbert, AZ 85233.

Credits

Our Journey Into Twilight, adapted from the article, "Muriel's Blessing," Robertson McQuilken, which first appeared in *Christianity Today*, February 5, 1996.

Fireproof, Marian Liautaud, first appeared in *Marriage Partnership*, Winter, 1996.

Resisting Temptation & Sustaining Life from *When Is It Right to Die?* Joni Eareckson Tada, Zondervan Publishing House, Michigan, 1992. Used by permission of publisher.

Dachau Chaplain from *Where is God When It Hurts*, Philip Yancey, Zondervan Publishing House, Michigan, 1977. Used by permission of publisher.

This Is A Test, Playing By The Rules & The Final Score of Trouble from *The Upside of Down*, Joseph M. Stowell, Moody Press, Illinois, 1991. Used by permission of publisher.

The Apron Strings, Perfect Shells and Broken Pieces & A Thousand Ways from *Rest Stops for Single Mothers*, Susan Titus Osborn and Lucille Moses, Broadman & Holman Publishers, Tennessee, 1995. Used by permission of publisher.

Showing Compassion & Forgiving God from *When Your Dreams Die*, Marilyn Willett Heavilin, Thomas Nelson, Tennessee, 1995. Used by permission of publisher.

Good-bye Again from *Weather of the Heart*, Gigi Graham Tchividjian, Multnomah Publishing, a division of Baker Book House Company, Michigan, 1986. Used by permission.

Grabbing Hold of Fulfillment, Unclaimed Gifts, & Depending On God from *Joy That Lasts*, Gary Smalley with Al Janssen, Zondervan, Michigan, 1986. Used by permission of publisher.

On the Anvil from *On the Anvil*, Max Lucado, Tyndale House Publishers, Inc. Illinois, 1985. Used by permission of publisher.

Waiting Had A Purpose from *A Graceful Waiting*, Jan Frank, Vine Books, (Servant Publications), Michigan, 1996. Used by permission of publisher.

Alone On A Saturday Night from *Common Mistakes Singles Make*, Mary Whelchel, Fleming H. Revell, a Division of Baker Book House, Michigan, 1989. Used by permission of publisher.

Flying First Class from *Abiding in Christ*, Cynthia Heald, Nav Press, Colorado, 1995. Used by permission of publisher.

Wounded Relationship from *Lord, Heal My Hurts*, Kay Arthur, Multomah, a division of Baker Book House, Michigan, 1988. Used by permission of publisher.

Fresh Elastic for Stretched Out Moms, Barbara Johnson, Fleming H. Revell, 1985.

Books by Starburst Publishers
(Partial listing—full list available on request)

God's Vitamin "C" for the Hurting Spirit
—Kathy Collard Miller & D. Larry Miller

The latest in the best-selling *God's Vitamin "C" for the Spirit* series, this collection of real-life stories expresses the breadth and depth of God's love for us in our times of need. Rejuvenating and inspiring thoughts from some of the most-loved Christian writers such as Max Lucado, Cynthia Heald, Gary Smalley, and Barbara Johnson. Topics include: Death, Divorce/Separation, Financial Loss, and Physical Illness.

(trade paper) ISBN 0914984691 **$12.95**

God's Vitamin "C" for the Spirit
—Kathy Collard Miller & D. Larry Miller

Subtitled: *"Tug-at-the-Heart" Stories to Fortify and Enrich Your Life.* Includes inspiring stories and anecdotes that emphasize Christian ideals and values by Barbara Johnson, Billy Graham, Nancy L. Dorner, Dave Dravecky, Patsy Clairmont, Charles Swindoll, H. Norman Wright, Adell Harvey, Max Lucado, James Dobson, Jack Hayford and many other well-known Christian speakers and writers. Topics include: Love, Family Life, Faith and Trust, Prayer, Marriage, Relationships, Grief, Spiritual Life, Perseverance, Christian Living, and God's Guidance.

(trade paper) ISBN 0914984837 **$12.95**

God's Chewable Vitamin "C" for the Spirit

Subtitled: *A Dose of God's Wisdom One Bite at a Time.* A collection of inspirational quotes and Scriptures by many of your favorite Christian speakers and writers. It will motivate your life and inspire your spirit. You will *chew* on every *bite* of *God's Chewable Vitamin "C" for the Spirit.*

(trade paper) ISBN 0914984845 **$6.95**

God's Vitamin "C" for the Spirit of WOMEN
—Kathy Collard Miller

Subtitled: *"Tug-at-the Heart" stories to Inspire and Delight Your Spirit.* A beautiful treasury of timeless stories, quotes and poetry designed by and for women. Well-known Christian women like Liz Curtis Higgs, Patsy Clairmont, Naomi Rhode and Elisabeth Elliott share from their hearts on subjects like Marriage, Motherhood, Christian Living, Faith and Friendship.

(trade paper) ISBN 0914984934 **$12.95**

God's Chewable Vitamin "C" for the Spirit of MOMs

Delightful, Insightful and Inspirational quotes combined with Scriptures that uplift and encourage women to succeed at the most important job in life—Motherhood.

(trade paper) ISBN 0914984942 **$6.95**

God's Vitamin "C" for the Spirit of MEN
—D. Larry Miller

Subtitled: *"Tug-at-the-Heart" Stories to Encourage and Strengthen Your Spirit.* Compiled in the format of best-selling *God's Vitamin "C" for the Spirit,* this book is filled with unique and inspiring stories that men of all ages will immediately relate to. True stories by some of the most-loved Christian speakers and writers on topics such as Integrity, Mentoring, Leadership, Marriage, Success/Failure, Family, Godliness, and Spiritual Life are sure to encourage men through the challenges of life. Contributors include Bill McCartney, Larry Crabb, Tim Kimmel, Billy Graham, Tony Evans, and R. C. Sproul, to name a few.

(trade paper) ISBN 0914984810 **$12.95**

Books by Starburst Publishers—cont'd.

God's Chewable Vitamin "C" for the Spirit of DADs

Subtitled: *A Dose of Godly Character, One Bite at a Time.* Scriptures coupled with insightful quotes to inspire men through the changes of life. This little "portable" is the perfect gift for men of all ages and walks of life. It provides the encouragement needed by Dad from time to time.

(trade paper) ISBN 0914984829 **$6.95**

God's Vitamin "C" for the Christmas Spirit
—Kathy Collard Miller & D. Larry Miller

Subtitled: *"Tug-at-the-Heart" Traditions and Inspirations to Warm the Heart.* Written in the same spirit as best-selling *God's Vitamin "C" for the Spirit,* this collection will rekindle new and old traditions for celebrating the Christmas season. This keepsake includes a variety of heart-tugging thoughts, stories, poetry, recipes, songs and crafts. Christian writers and speakers, such as Pat Boone, Cheri Fuller, Gloria Gaither, Joni Eareckson, and Michael Card combine their talents to produce a book that is sure to encourage a time of peace, relaxation, and the building of your own cherished Christmas memories.

(hardcover) ISBN 0914984853 **$14.95**

The Miracle of the Sacred Scroll
—Johan Christian

In this poignant book, Johan Christian masterfully weaves historical and biblical reality together with a touching fictional story to bring to life this marvelous work—a story that takes its main character, Simon of Cyrene, on a journey which transforms his life, and that of the reader, from one of despair and defeat to success and triumph!

(hardcover) ISBN 091498473X **$14.95**

God's Abundance
—Edited by Kathy Collard Miller

Subtitled: *365 Days to a Simpler Life.* This day-by-day inspirational is a collection of thoughts by leading Christian writers such as, Patsy Clairmont, Jill Briscoe, Liz Curtis Higgs and Robert Schuller. *God's Abundance* is based on God's Word for a simpler, yet more abundant life. Similar in style to the best-seller, *Simple Abundance,* but with a biblical basis. Most people think more about the future while the present passes through their hands. Learn to make all aspects of your life—personal, business, financial, relationships, even housework be a "spiritual abundance of simplicity."

(hardcover) ISBN 0914984977 **$19.95**

Revelation—God's Word for the Biblically-Inept
—Daymond Duck

Revelation—God's Word for the Biblically-Inept is the first in a new series designed to make understanding and learning the Bible as easy and fun as learning your ABC's. Reading the Bible is one thing, understanding it is another! This book breaks down the barrier of difficulty and helps take the Bible off the pedestal and into your hands.

(trade paper) ISBN 0914984985 **$16.95**

The Frazzled Working Woman's Practical Guide to Motherhood
—Mary Lyon

It's Emma Bombeck meets Martha Stewart meets cartoonist Cathy Guisewite. The author's extensive original cartoon illustrations further enliven a sparklingly humorous narrative, making her a new James Thurber! *Frazzled* is an essential companion for any working woman who thinks she wants a baby, or is currently expecting one. Especially if she could use a good laugh to lighten her load and her worries. This book also offers an innovative update on effective working-mom strategies to women who are already off and running on the "Mommy Track."

(trade paper) ISBN 0914984756 **$14.95**

Books by Starburst Publishers—cont'd.

Baby Steps to Success   —Vince Lombardi Jr. & John Q. Baucom

Subtitled: *52 Vince Lombardi-Inspired Ways to Make Your Life Successful.* Vince Lombardi's is one of the most quoted success stories in the history of the world. From corporate boardrooms to athletic locker rooms, his wisdom is studied, read, and posted on walls. The same skills that Coach Lombardi used to turn the Green Bay Packers from cellar dwellers to world champions is now available to you in *Baby Steps To Success.* This book can help you be more successful in your career, personal or family life. The same principles that made the Packers Super Bowl champions can make you a "Super Bowl" employee, parent or spouse. These principles are broken down into 52 unique and achievable "Baby Steps."

(trade paper) ISBN 0914984950   **$12.95**

Little Baby Steps to Success

Subtitled: *Vince Lombardi's Motivational Wisdom and Insight to Make Your Life Successful.* Motivational, inspiring and filled with insight that will get you off the bench and into the game of success. This wisdom-filled, pocket-sized collection of the best of Lombardi will help you one small step at a time to reach the goals you have imagined.

(trade paper) ISBN 0914984969   **$6.95**

Baby Steps to Happiness   —John Q. Baucom

Subtitled: *52 Inspiring Ways to Make Your Life Happy.* This unique 52-step approach will enable the reader to focus on small steps that bring practical and proven change. The author encourages the reader to take responsibility for the Happiness that only he can find. Chapter titles, such as, *Have a Reason to Get Out of Bed, Deal with Your Feelings or Become Them, Would You Rather Be Right or Happy?* and *Love To Win More Than You Hate to Lose* give insight and encouragement on the road to happiness.

(trade paper) ISBN 0914984861   **$12.95**

Little Baby Steps to Happiness   —John Q. Baucom

Inspiring, witty and insightful, this portable collection of quotes and affirmations from *Baby Steps to Happiness* will encourage Happiness one little footstep at a time. This book is the perfect personal "cheerleader."

(trade paper) ISBN 091498487X   **$6.95**

Grapes of Righteousness   —Joseph H. Powell

Subtitled: *Spiritual Grafting Into the True Vine.* Dr. Powell uses an analogy that compares and contrasts our development into God's kingdom under His hands, to the cultivating and nurturing of a vineyard by a gardener. Possessing a Ph.D in Botany, the author uses his extensive study of grafting, pruning, nutrition, and dormancy to illustrate the basic Biblical principles necessary to spiritual birth and subsequent growth and maturity.

(trade paper) ISBN 0914984748   **$10.95**

God Is!   —Mark R. Littleton

"Heart-Tugging" inspirational stories, quotes & illustrations that will leave a powerful mental and emotional impact on the reader. Short and easy-to-read sketches, embracing the attributes of God, will inspire your spirit and brighten your day. Topics include, *God Is Love, God Is Good, God Is Wise* and more.

(hardcover) ISBN 0914984926   **$14.95**

Books by Starburst Publishers—cont'd.

The Remnant —Gilbert Morris

How far will the New Age philosophy with it's "politically correct" doctrine take us? *The Remnant*, the second futuristic novel in The Far Fields series, continues the story which began in *Beyond the River*—that of a world where a total authoritarian government has replaced family and rewritten history.

(trade paper) ISBN 0914984918 **$8.95**

Beyond The River —Gilbert Morris & Bobby Funderburk

Book 1 in The Far Fields series is a a futuristic novel that carries the New Age and "politically correct" doctrines of America to their logical and alarming conclusions. In the mode of *Brave New World* and *1984*, *Beyond The River* presents a world where government has replaced the family and morality has become an unknown concept.

(trade paper) ISBN 0914984519 **$8.95**

Parenting With Respect and Peacefulness —Louise A. Dietzel

Subtitled: *The Most Difficult Job in the World*. Parents who love and respect themselves parent with respect and peacefulness. Yet, parenting with respect is the most difficult job in the world. This book informs parents that respect and peace communicate love—creating an atmosphere for children to maximize their development as they feel loved, valued, and safe. Parents learn authority and control by a common sense approach to day-to-day situations in parenting.

(trade paper) ISBN 0914984667 **$10.95**

A Woman's Guide To Spiritual Power —Nancy L. Dorner

Subtitled: *Through Scriptural Prayer*. Do your prayers seem to go "against a brick wall?" Does God sometimes seem far away or non-existent? If your answer is "Yes," you are not alone. Prayer must be the cornerstone of your relationship to God. "This book is a powerful tool for anyone who is serious about prayer and discipleship." —Florence Littauer

(trade paper) ISBN 0914984470 **$9.95**

Purchasing Information:

Books are available from your favorite bookstore, either from current stock or special order. To assist bookstore in locating your selection be sure to give title, author, and ISBN #. If unable to purchase from the bookstore you may order direct from STARBURST PUBLISHERS. When ordering enclose full payment plus $3.00 for shipping and handling ($4.00 if Canada or Overseas). Payment in US Funds only. Please allow two to three weeks minimum (longer overseas) for delivery. Make checks payable to and mail to STARBURST PUBLISHERS, P.O. Box 4123, LANCASTER, PA 17604. Credit card orders may also be placed by calling 1-800-441-1456 (credit card orders only), Mon-Fri, 8:30 a.m. – 5:30 p.m. Eastern Time. **Prices subject to change without notice.** Catalog available for a 9 x 12 self-addressed envelope with 4 first-class stamps. 11-97